I asked several former students of [   ] *San Jose Christian College) if they wo* [   ] *so grateful for their kind responses.*

"Les' new book is just what's needed to get ministry out of the rut of closed-minded thinking and open to a world of possibility. This book will show you how to release God to work in and through your life."

—Nathan L. Cherry, children's pastor, Westside Christian Church, Roseville, California

"Les shares why creativity matters and how each of us is created to be creative. He also gives us very practical ways to keep the creativity flowing in our ministries."

—Justin Humphreys, student pastor, Spring Creek Community Church, Garland, Texas

"*Awaken Your Creativity* will strike a flame in the heart of any youth worker wanting to be free from the norm. I pray that these pages inspire you to be different, as they have inspired me. A must-read for any pastor or youth worker who wants to connect with their students."

—Russ Cantu, student pastor, Prescott Church, Modesto, California

"Creativity in youth ministry is essential. It helps us weave our way through the many obstacles we encounter and allows us to see new perspectives within old ways of working with youth. *Awaken Your Creativity* will enhance your inner creativity, refresh your excitement for reaching and retaining youth, and offer practical tools in a fun, easy read."

—Jacqi-Rae Kambish, Saint Timothy's Lutheran Church, San Jose, California

"Les' book is an encouragement to anyone who struggles with their God-given creativity, especially us left-brained folks! In ministry, it's easiest to find the pattern that works best and perpetuate it. Les shows how detrimental this thinking can be and how important it is to tap into that piece of the image of God called *creativity*."

—Forrest Thomas, youth pastor, Sebastopol (California) Christian Church

LES CHRISTIE

AWAKEN YOUR CREATIVITY

Hearing Yes in the Midst of a Multitude of No's

YOUTH SPECIALTIES

Awaken Your Creativity: Hearing Yes in the Midst of a Multitude of No's
Copyright 2009 by Les Christie

Youth Specialties resources, 1890 Cordell Ct. Ste. 105, El Cajon, CA 92020 are published by Zondervan, 5300 Patterson Ave. SE, Grand Rapids, MI 49530.

ISBN 978-0-310-28778-0

Cover design by Invisible Creature
Interior design by Mark Novelli, IMAGO-MEDIA

Printed in the United States of America

09 10 11 12 13 14 • 20 19 18 17 16 15 14 13 12 11 10 9 8 7 6 5 4 3 2 1

DEDICATION

This book is dedicated to two of the many creative people who have influenced and molded my life. Both of these men always encouraged me to ask questions and to be curious.

My grandfather, Walter Christie, worked for 20th Century Fox studios for more than 30 years. He was a journeyman grip who built the sets for many movies and television programs. As a young boy I remember going to the marina and watching him take the hull of a whaling ship and transform it over many months into a beautiful boat. My grandfather lived to be 96 and spent some of his later years on that boat.

I also want to recognize the creativity of my father, Les Arthur Christie, who is still going strong at age 88. He was a machinist who worked more than 30 years for the same company, securing many patents for that company. If you walk around my parents' home, you can't help but see all kinds of electrical inventions, mechanical gadgets, musical instruments, and works of art that he and my mom have created or collected to enhance their days and make their lives simpler. To this day, my parents can never pass up a garage sale, swap meet, or flea market.

CONTENTS

ACKNOWLEDGMENTS

I want to thank Craig McNair Wilson, who was the first person I'd ever heard give a talk on creativity. He inspired me to consider other ways of looking at everyday objects.

I also want to thank Mike Yaconelli, who asked me to contribute to his book, *The CORE Realities of Youth Ministry*, specifically the chapter on creativity. You'll find ideas that appeared in that chapter throughout this book. Mike was the first one to encourage me to put my ideas about creativity into print.

I want to express my gratitude to our academic dean at William Jessup University, David Nystrom, who encouraged the entire faculty to read *The Medici Effect.* That book encouraged my own interest in the topic of creativity and prompted me to read a lot more on the subject.

I want to thank Thom and Joani Schultz of Group Publishing who asked me to give a seminar on creativity at their national conference. I also want to thank David Welch, who heard that seminar and suggested I present that material at the YS conventions. I'm also grateful to both David and Jay Howver at YS for encouraging me to write this book.

I am so grateful for the competent team of people at YS/Zondervan who worked on the details of this book. There's always a little trepidation when an author hands over a manuscript to a group of people he's not necessarily met. I was so happy to learn that Doug Davidson would again be my editor. I have full confidence in his ability to help shape my thoughts and get them on paper. He's been a pleasure to work with. I am also indebted to and appreciative of Dave Urbanski, senior developmental editor, for stepping in at the last moment to help bring this book to completion. I am also thankful to David Conn for his design of the book cover, which captured the look I was hoping for, and to Mark Novelli for his interior layout. I'd also like to thank Roni Meek who has been very helpful throughout the publishing process.

INTRODUCTION

I wrote this book with the goal of bringing new enthusiasm to your life and ministry. I hope you'll find that it makes you laugh and challenges your thinking. As you read, my desire is that you would discover how very creative you really are.

Awaken Your Creativity will help you discover what hinders you from releasing your God-given creativity—and help you find ways to overcome those barriers. You'll learn to identify and remove the stumbling blocks that often keep us from being the creative people God designed us to be. You'll uncover some of the tricks of the trade and shortcuts imaginative people often use. You'll learn the catalysts that trigger inventiveness, and master new ways to tap into both your own creativity and the creativity of your team and others around you.

I sometimes ask attendees at my conferences and seminars to give me words that describe someone who has a creative ministry. Here is a sample of what they have come up with:

- Challenging
- Outrageous
- Life-giving
- Original
- Extreme
- Unique
- Invigorating

- Exceptional
- New
- Imaginative
- Fresh
- Distinctive
- Fun
- Innovative

- Personal
- Enjoyable
- Exciting
- Inventive
- Unexpected
- Inspired
- Genuine

When I ask people what words come to mind when they think of a ministry that is uncreative, they offer the following words:

- Boring
- Dull
- Uninteresting
- Unexciting
- Mind numbing
- Tedious
- Monotonous
- Tiresome
- Stagnant

- Conformist
- Dry
- Conventional
- Traditional
- Dreary
- Humdrum
- Fixed
- Mundane
- Redundant

- Inactive
- Stationary
- Dormant
- Outmoded
- Traditional
- Repetitious
- Unimaginative
- Cookie Cutter

So which list is the better description of your life and ministry? Which describes what you want your ministry to be? If you're comfortable describing your ministry with the words on the second list, put this book down because it will drive you nuts. But if the first list looks appealing, then continue reading—because this book will help you on the road to getting there.

It's my desire that you will go away from this book feeling confident and enthused about how original, clever, and resourceful you are. I hope you'll find yourself looking at the same information everyone else is viewing, yet you'll see something different. You'll discover new ideas and have unique insights.

This book will change how you perceive your own creativity, while stripping creativity of its mystique. You will, perhaps for the first time, see endless possibilities stretching before you. You will learn how to:

- Generate ideas
- Create new ministry opportunities
- Manipulate and modify ideas to find the most novel possibilities
- Improve old ways of doing ministry
- Develop new and innovative solutions to difficult ministry dilemmas
- Become more productive
- See problems as opportunities
- Become the "idea person" in your ministry
- Know where to look for the "breakthrough idea"

I think you'll find *Awaken Your Creativity* to be an enjoyable read. It's packed with stories that will bring a smile to your face, as well as practical hints you can use in your day-to-day ministry. I trust it will help you get back to the kid inside you. I hope you walk away from this book with a new vitality to your life and ministry with an energy that endures.

YOU ARE A CREATIVE PERSON

CHAPTER ONE

Most people go through life without ever knowing how creative they really are. How sad is that?

I believe every single one of us one has incredible creative potential—and it's possible for anyone to discover his or her hidden creativity. Creativity is about the full and complete expression of your identity in Christ. It is about releasing the creative nature God has placed within each of us.

Creativity is the ability to bring something new into existence by using one's imagination, ingenuity, and inventiveness. It's also one of God's primary characteristics. In the very first pages of Scripture, we learn of how God created the world—and then created humans in his own image. Because we are made in the image of God, the God who invented creativity, we are creative as well—all of us. If you say you are not creative, you are denying God's stamp on your soul.

I believe an effective youth ministry is one that helps teenagers rediscover their creativity. The youth group should be known for its originality, freshness, and resourcefulness. It should be the breeding place of wonder, passion, and unpredictability. It should be a place where your students are helped to find and fulfill the unique purposes God has for each of them.

The youth ministry should also be a place where your uniqueness finds expression. Trust your uniqueness. Why? Because what makes you different is the result of God's creativity. Each of us is unusual, unique, one of a kind. Each of us has different gifts, weaknesses, and specialties. Each of us works with different students who all have their own needs and strengths. Many youth ministry models are franchised or copied, and finding ideas that have worked for others can be a good place to start. But in order to allow our creativity to work, we need to recognize our own unique qualities. Our individual perspectives and gifts make our ministries a true reflection of the Holy Spirit in us.

It is easy to find yourself in a rut. When this takes place, our creative side can get pushed aside. Too many youth workers are like the caterpillars that French naturalist Jean-Henri Fabre (1823-1915) spent most of his life studying. Fabre was a reclusive amateur with no scientific training, yet he was an acute observer of insect behavior, often in his own backyard.

Fabre was fascinated by processionary caterpillars. They feed on pine needles and leafy plants, and often move along tree branches in long processions (hence the name). Each caterpillar marches with its eyes half closed and its head down and tucked closely to the rear extremity of the caterpillar before it. Dozens of them march in such a line as a single unit.

One day Fabre decided to play a little joke on them. He managed to entice them to walk from a tree branch to the top rim of a large flower pot. As the caterpillars walked around the rim of the pot, eventually the lead caterpillar ran into the end of the line. The lead caterpillar then put its head snuggly up against the rear end of the last caterpillar and continued the procession, which was now circling the rim of the pot with no beginning or end. Fabre thought they would catch on to his little joke at any time, stop circling, and walk off the pot in some new direction—but they didn't. Instead, by sheer force of habit they kept moving around the rim of the flower pot. Around and

I spent 22 years as a full-time youth minister at a church in Fullerton, California, and I was fortunate to have a lot of wonderful volunteers who worked on our youth ministry staff. One of the most memorable was a man named Forrest Bright. Forrest worked with his hands most of his life. A carpenter by trade, he'd built some fine homes in the Orange County area, and I admired him before I really knew him. He was a quiet man who often spent his weekends doing various repair and construction jobs for families in need.

One day he asked if he could work with the youth. He said he didn't want to stand in front of a group and speak, nor did he want to lead a small discussion group of students. Yet he felt God calling him to work with teenagers in some way.

I asked if he would allow some of our teens to assist him on the weekends when he did repairs for those in need. He agreed, and for the next two years, he had several young men and women assisting him. A few of them even went on to become full-time carpenters themselves. I think those students learned more from a weekend of watching this large, gentle man with a big heart minister to people than they did from a dozen of my talks. God used Forrest's abilities to provide a creative ministry for the students as well as those they helped.

You may not know Forrest, but I bet you've heard of his younger brother—Bill Bright, founder of Campus Crusade for Christ. While the success of Bill's ministry is undeniable, I've always admired how Forrest used the unique gifts and creativity God had given to him. Sometimes I wonder who really had the most successful ministry!

YOU ARE A CREATIVE PERSON

around they went for several days. They eventually died from starvation and exhaustion even though there was food and water nearby.

Sometimes our ministries get in this same type of routine. We blindly follow those who have gone before us, or the way we've always done it. We bury our heads and continue doing everything the same old way—even when it is not working anymore.

"Imagination is more important than knowledge."

EINSTEIN

"Mental constipation occurs when you have old ideas in your head that prevent you from having new ideas and entertaining alternative points of view. The thing to do is flush out the old ideas."

DOUG HALL, *JUMP START YOUR BRAIN*

If we want our ministries to thrive and grow, we can't get locked up in old formations, old models, old perceptions, and old observations. For many ministries it is time to think outside of the box, color outside of the lines, and break out of the mold. It is time to take a risk and try something different.

GETTING STARTED

Try this. Put your fists up against your ears. Now move your left fist out so it's about three feet from your left ear. Then, as you move your right fist away from your right ear, pull your left fist closer to your left ear. Go back and forth, moving your fist close to and then away from your ears. This is called mental flossing. I hope you are willing to unclog your brain and get rid of misconceptions about the way things have to be done so you can open yourself to new ideas and your own creativity!

One way to open our thinking is to allow God to free up our brains. Romans 12:2 (NLT) tells us, "Let God transform you into a new person by changing the way you think." John 8:32 adds, "You will know the truth, and the truth will set you free."

I hear some youth leaders say creativity is a natural gift that cannot be taught or learned. They say either you're creative or you're not—and there's nothing you can do about it. They often support this argument by pointing to extreme cases of creativity. They talk about Las Vegas shows like Cirque

du Soliel or Penn and Teller, and say, "I could never do that. I'm just not creative." You may never be Tiger Woods, but that should not stop you from playing golf. We don't give up teaching people to play the piano or violin because we cannot guarantee that every student will be Chopin or Midori.

That some people are extremely creative and talented does not mean they would not be even more creative with some training and techniques. Nor does it mean other people can never become creative. We are all born with creative gifts, and we can all develop and nurture those gifts.

We often think creativity means breaking every rule and going against all expectations. But as Edward de Bono points out in *Serious Creativity*, working within a system successfully also requires creativity:

> At school the more intelligent youngsters seem to be conformists. They quickly learn the "game" that is required: How to please the teacher. How to pass exams with minimal effort...In this way they ensure a peaceful life and the ability to get on with what really interests them.

Then there are the rebels. The rebels, for reasons of temperament or the need to be noticed, do not want to play the going game. It is only natural to assume that in later life creativity is going to have to come from the rebels. The conformists are busily learning the appropriate games, playing them, and adjusting to them. So it is up to the rebels to challenge existing concepts and to set out to do things differently. The rebels have the courage, the energy, and the different points of view.

"Toto, something tells me we're not in Kansas anymore."

DOROTHY IN *THE WIZARD OF OZ* (MGM, 1939)

Gordon MacKenzie compares creativity to vitreous floaters—those little, hair-like squiggles that exist in our eyeballs that we sometimes see floating randomly across our fields of vision. He writes:

"Have you ever noticed: If you look right at them—the squiggles, I mean—they go off to the side! Right out of view if you keep staring at them. And have you noticed, too, if you want them to return, all you have to do is stop looking at them. If you do that—stop looking at them—very gradually, they'll float back into your line of sight. It's almost as if they're shy. Stare at them, and they'll go away. Look the other way, and, silently, they will reappear. Creativity is like that. It will not be looked at. As soon as you look at creativity—as soon as you become conscious (or self-conscious) of it—it simply vanishes. If you want it to return, you must give up trying to focus on it."

GORDON RAY MACKENZIE, *ORBITING THE GIANT HAIRBALL*

YOU ARE A CREATIVE PERSON

15

This is our traditional view of creativity. But it could be changing.

Once we begin to understand the nature of creativity...then we can start laying out the "game" and the steps in the game. Once society decides that this game is worth playing and should be rewarded then we might well get the "conformists" deciding that they want to play this new "game." So conformists learn the game of creativity.... The conformists might soon become more creative than the rebels who do not want to learn or play any games.

So we might get the strange paradox that the conformists actually become more creative than the rebels. I think this is beginning to happen....

> "Years back, a group of scientists visited a tribe in New Guinea that believed their world ended at a nearby river. After several months, one of the scientists had to leave, which involved crossing the river. Safely across the river, he turned around and waved. The tribesmen did not respond because, they said, they didn't see him. Their entrenched beliefs about the world had distorted their perception of reality."
>
> MICHAEL MICHALKO, *TINKERTOYS*

The rebel often achieves creativity by striking out against the prevailing ideas and going against current idioms. The momentum of the rebel is obtained by being "against" something. But the creativity of conformists...does not need to be "against" anything— so it can be more constructive and can also build on existing ideas. So creativity is certainly not restricted to rebels but creative skills can be acquired even by those who have always considered themselves conformists.

Remember that creativity in ministry is not an end to itself. Adult youth leaders should not be creative for creativity's sake. Mike Yaconelli once pointed out that creativity "is not a novelty or an attempt to impress others. Usually, ideas developed without any goal in mind simply because they're creative don't work well. The purpose of creativity is to make what we're doing or saying more helpful, useful, and effective."

AWAKENING YOUR CREATIVITY

YOUR AMAZING BRAIN

The human brain is extraordinary. It weighs only three pounds and is the size of a small cantaloupe. It is lightening fast, adaptive, clever, and can tell if something is wrong with it.

Brain development begins in the first month after conception. The developing brain includes two types of cells: Neurons, which talk to one another and to the rest of the body; and glial cells, which provide essential support to keep the whole thing going. Within six months of conception, most of the billions of neurons that populate the mature brain have been created. Every minute, more than 250,000 new neurons are being generated and even more glial cells. Together they forge an

> "I used to think my brain was my most important organ. But then I thought: *Wait a minute, who's telling me that?*"
>
> EMO PHILLIPS, COMEDIAN

elaborate network of some one *quadrillion* (1,000,000,000,000,000) connections that guide how we talk, eat, breathe, and move. James Watson, who won the Nobel Prize for helping discover DNA, described the human brain as "the most complex thing we have yet discovered in our universe." Woody Allen called the brain "my second favorite organ."

The human brain has three basic units: The forebrain, midbrain, and hindbrain. The seat of all thought and reasoning is the cerebrum, which is positioned right behind the brow in the forebrain. This section of the brain houses the ability to plan, imagine, read, recognize friends and acquaintances, and store short-term memory, which makes it possible to consider a new idea without forgetting concepts previously entertained.

Although our brains reach 90 percent of their adult size by the time we are six, there's a lot going on during that last 10 percent of growth. Some of the last connections to be formed are in the prefrontal cortex, a brain region that is important in moral reasoning and planning for the future. Adolescents may be only partway down the road toward having a fully functional set of prefrontal connections, which may explain why teens go through more emotional turmoil, have poor impulse control, and are more likely to take risks compared to those who are older. We find this not only in humans but also in animals.

There has long been a rumor floating around that we only use 10 percent of our brains. That is not true. The myth was originally attributed to

William James, but no one has found the 10 percent figure in his writings or speeches. But regardless of who came up with this idea, it's simply not true. We all use our whole brain every single day.

Scientist Eric Kandel, who shared in the Nobel Prize in 2000, says our brains are constantly learning and constantly rewiring themselves. No two brains are wired identically. Because each brain is as unique as a fingerprint, we have to remember that the brains of students in our youth ministries are each wired differently. This fact alone should be enough to motivate you to provide small-group opportunities for your students if you have more than 10 kids in your ministry. Groups of three to eight students allow the adult youth leaders to really keep track all their students.

When a neurosurgeon is preparing to operate on someone's brain, the surgeon must first map that individual's brain. While the patient is partially awake on the operating table, the doctor will touch parts of the brain with a wire that sends a mild electric shock and then ask the patient if he/she felt anything. In this way the surgeon identifies various functions of the patient's brain surrounding the area where the surgery will take place. For example, if someone is bilingual the French language may be in a different place than the English language. Nouns and verbs may be in separate places. Feelings in arms and legs may be in different places. Surgeons know the general places where functions of our bodies are controlled, but the specific spots can vary between individuals—so this mind mapping must be done with each patient.

Another amazing thing about our brains is the way they build up patterns that enable us to simplify, survive, and cope with a complex world based on our experiences that have been successful in the past. For example, we look at 8 x 8 and the number 64 appears automatically, without conscious thought.

For the last 20 years a story has been circulating about a word study that was said to have originated at Cambridge University. The study itself seems to be bogus, a hoax. I've never found anyone who could confirm that this study was ever done at Cambridge or anywhere else. But it is still an interesting illustration of the ability of our brains to form patterns and sort out words. Here's one version:

> Aoccdrnig to rsceearh at Cmabrigde Uinervtisy, it deosn't mttaer in waht oredr the ltteers in a wrod are, the olny iprmoatnt tihng is taht the frist and lsat ltteer be in the rghit pclae. The rset can be

a taotl mses and you can sitll raed it wouthit a porbelm. Tihs is bcuseae the huamn mnid deos not raed ervey lteter by istlef, but the wrod as a wlohe.

Even though the study never happened, the statement itself is interesting. The concept breaks down when the words are longer and harder, and the context is less obvious. But it is still fascinating what our minds are capable of doing.

Our brains are capable of filling in the blanks for us. Check out the following drawing:

What do you see? Our brains search for something we have seen previously that is similar to these blotches of black ink and fills in the missing spaces.

Or take a look at this next drawing. Do you see the circles? Most people do, but there aren't any circles.

But there's one problem with this amazing ability we have to develop and recognize patterns: This same thinking that makes it easy to identify and make use of information we've seen before can make it harder for us to come up with new ideas and creative solutions to problems. When we sit down and try to find new solutions, we tend to keep coming up with the same old ideas. Or, to put it another way, if you always think what you've always thought, you'll always get what you've always got. Creativity demands that we break out of our old thought patterns.

LEFT BRAIN AND RIGHT BRAIN

Before we move on, let's look at how one other aspect of our brains affects creativity. When people talk about "right brain" and "left brain," they are referring to the two sides of the cortex, each of which has different functions. Scientists first learned about these functions by studying people with brain damage, including soldiers who'd been wounded in battle. Soldiers who survived head wounds exhibited a wide range of symptoms, which varied depending on the location of the wound and the portion of the brain that was damaged.

These studies determined that our verbal abilities, as well as our math and logic skills, are concentrated in the left cerebral hemisphere. The left side seems to have an intense need for logic and order; it processes information rationally and linearly. Most schools train us to use our left side of our brain.

The right side contains non-rational information. It thinks: *What a beautiful sunset!* or *Wouldn't it be neat if we could live in a giant cleaned-out pumpkin?* In school, the right brain is often told to be quiet. The right brain is more open to creative ideas, while the left brain asks *What will that idea cost?*

Michael Michalko points out our minds are incredible connection-making and connection-recognizing machines. He suggests trying this experiment:

Pick eight random words and give the list to someone or to a small group (for example: "flowerpot," "baby," "glass," "grasshopper," "coffeepot," "box," "toast," and "garage"). Ask them to divide the words into two groups without giving them any rationale for the division. You'll discover that people will come up with some very creative classifications. They'll group them according to "words with the letter o," "things that touch water," "objects made in factories," and so on. No one ever says there is no connection.

MICHAEL MICHALKO, *CRACKING CREATIVITY*

Men tend to be more left-brain focused than women. But we all need to use both sides of our brain to function well in society. And all of us can learn to make more effective use of the less dominant side of our brains.

There's some debate among scientists about what side of the brain is responsible for creativity. Some studies have determined that the right hemisphere is more responsible for visual artistry than any other region; other studies have suggested that the talents of great artists emanate from multiple parts of the brain; and still other researchers have suggested that the creative impulse may be a consequence of antagonistic interaction between the strongly connected temporal lobes.

YOU ARE A CREATIVE PERSON

But whether creativity emanates from the right brain, the left brain, or some interaction between the two, one thing is clear: For those of us in youth ministry, *being creative is the right thing to do*. In the chapters that follow, we'll look at how you can enhance your own creative impulses so that you can be more effective in reaching and ministering to students.

SO-NOT-DONE QUESTIONS

1. Where do you see God's creativity in the world around us? How is it revealed in the Scriptures?

2. When you think of a creative person, who comes to mind?

3. Do you agree with Einstein's statement, "Imagination is more important than knowledge"? Why or why not?

4. What do you find amazing about your brain?

5. Are you more a right or left brain person? Are you okay with this?

6. When have you found creativity to be elusive?

7. What areas of your life and ministry are most in need of change and renewed creativity?

BARRIERS TO CREATIVITY

So what keeps us from being creative? What stops us from taking risks? What keeps us from trying new things? What causes us to leave our God-given creativity back on the shelf? Let me suggest a few possibilities.

WE LOST OUR INNOCENCE

Robert Fulghum, author of *All I Really Need to Know I Learned in Kindergarten*, tells of speaking to a kindergarten class and asking a series of questions:

"How many of you can draw?" he asked. All hands shot up.

"How many of you can sing?" Again, all hands.

"How many of you can dance?" Unanimous.

"How many of you can act in plays?" YES! YES! YES! YES!

The young kids answered YES to every question—over and over again. Everything is possible at that age.

Try asking those same questions of the students at the university where I teach, and only a few will raise their hands. Or they'll qualify their responses with "I don't have that talent" or "I'm not majoring in the subject" or "I haven't done those things since third grade." For the most part, if you ask those same questions of an older audience, you'll hear a resounding "no."

Young children are not inhibited by the constraints of what people say cannot be done, so they are free to suggest inventive thoughts. But we often lose that ability as we grow older.

A teacher asked a four-year-old what she was drawing. She responded, "I am drawing God." The teacher said, "No one knows what God looks like." The child replied, "They will in a minute!"

"The key question," Abraham Maslow declared, "isn't 'What fosters creativity?' It is, 'Why isn't everyone creative? Where was the human potential lost? How was it crippled?' I think a good question might be not, 'Why do people create?' but 'Why do people not create or innovate?' We have got to abandon the sense of amazement in the face of creativity, as if it were a miracle if anybody created anything."

So again I ask: What happened to us? What went wrong between kindergarten and adulthood? What happened to "YES!"?

Somewhere along the line, we stopped playing house, singing, and dancing. We learned that elephants don't have wings and trees don't have stripes. We were told there are correct and not correct things to think, feel, and say.

In the Austin Powers film series, Dr. Evil (Mike Myers) keeps interrupting his son, Scotty, as the young man tries to express his ideas. Dr. Evil does this by continually saying "shush." Dr. Evil tells his son that he has a "bag full of shushes." In life we meet a lot of Dr. Evils who keep telling us just to sit still and be quiet.

So what should we do? First, get in touch with the child inside you. Close your eyes and imagine yourself at your most inquisitive age. Perhaps you can imagine yourself at ten years of age— or maybe younger. Experience the joy of possibilities; the encouragement of friends, parents, teachers, and pastors; the wonder of Thanksgivings, Christmases, Fourths of July, and birthdays.

Picasso once remarked, "All children are artists." He said he became a true artist only when he learned how to paint like a child. Perhaps, on certain occasions, we should actually ask a few children how they would handle a problem—and then really listen to them.

CREATIVITY WAS EDUCATED OUT OF US

There is a hierarchy in education. Subjects like math, science, English, and history are near the top. Things like band, drama, and the arts are at the bottom. We are all born as spontaneous, creative thinkers. Yet a great deal of our education seems designed to teach us "what" to think instead of "how" to think. Each of us enters school as a question mark but graduate as a period.

Little children tend to be naturally creative, but often our creativity is educated out of us. If children are allowed to remain curious, they will continue to utilize their natural tendencies to discover and explore until they are past 100. For children creativity and discovery brings joy. But there are constraints in the educational systems that continue to maintain traditional approaches to teaching even when they are not working.

"My 2-year-old son, Noah, and I were walking down the street on our way to preschool when he suddenly noticed a shinny pebble embedded in the concrete. Stopping mid-stride, the little guy considered it for a second, found it thoroughly delightful, and let out a laugh. He spied a small plant an inch farther, a weed valiantly struggling through a crack in the asphalt. He touched it gently and then laughed again. Noah noticed beyond it a platoon of ants marching in a single file, which he bent down to examine closely. They were carrying a dead bug, and Noah clapped his hands in wonder. There were dust particles, a rusted screw, and a shiny spot of oil. Fifteen minutes had passed, and we had gone only 20 feet. I tried to get him to move along, having the audacity to act like an adult with a schedule. He was having none of it. And I stopped, watching my little teacher, wondering how long it had been since I had taken 15 minutes to walk 20 feet."

JOHN MEDINA, *BRAIN RULES*

"Never let formal education get in the way of your learning."

MARK TWAIN

In *Jump Start Your Brain*, Doug Hall suggests ten ways to restore a spirit of innocence:

- Inhale the contents of a helium balloon, then speak over the intercom system

- Climb a tree

- Fly a kite

- Hang by your knees from the monkey bars

- Swing as high as you can

- Roll down a hill

- Spin until dizzy

- Take a different route to work or school

- Have dinner at the ninth restaurant listed in the yellow pages

- Ask the fifth person you talk to at work to go to lunch that day

Another reason we're not more creative is that we haven't been taught to be. Jean Piaget once said that the principal goal of education should be to create men and women who are capable of doing new things, rather than simply repeating what other generations have done. Yet many of us have been taught that the best ideas are in someone else's head. Many classroom discussions are just an elaborate game of "guess what the teacher is thinking." How many of your teachers ever asked, "What original ideas do you have?" (And, by the way, this is also true of the church.)

As we grow older we encounter life's experiences, and they tend to make us more "realistic"—and that's not necessarily a good thing. Consequently, we tend to process information the same way and do the same things over and over, instead of searching for alternatives. Once we think we know what works or what can be done, it becomes difficult for us to consider other possibilities. Even when we seek ways to test our ideas to see if we are right, we often ignore paths that might lead us to discover alternatives.

The following story from Mary Schramm's *Gifts of Grace* illustrates this principle:

> Once a little boy went to school. It was quite a big school, but when the boy found he could go right to his room from the playground outside he was happy, and the school didn't seem quite so big anymore. One morning when the little boy had been in school for a while, the teacher said, "Today we are going to make a picture."
>
> "Good," thought the little boy. He liked to make pictures. He could make lions and tigers and trains and boats. He took out his

crayons and began to draw. But the teacher said, "Wait. It's not the time to begin." And she waited until everyone looked ready. "Now," said the teacher, "we are going to make flowers."

"Good," thought the little boy, and he began to make beautiful flowers with his orange and pink and blue crayons. But the teacher said, "Wait." She drew a picture on the blackboard. It was red with a green stem. "There, now you may begin."

The little boy looked at the teacher's flower. He liked his better, but he did not say this. He just turned his paper over and made a flower like the teacher's. It was red with a green stem.

On another day, the teacher said, "Today we are going to make something with clay." "Good," thought the little boy. He could make all kinds of things with clay—snakes and snowmen and elephants and mice—and he began to pinch and pull his ball of clay. But again the teacher said, "Wait, I'll show you how." And she showed everyone how to make one deep dish. The little boy just rolled his clay in a round ball and made a dish like the teacher's. And pretty soon the little boy learned to wait and to watch and to make things just like the teacher's. And pretty soon he didn't make things of his own anymore.

And then it happened that the little boy and his parents moved to another city and the boy had to go to another school. On the very first day he went to school the teacher said, "Today we are going to make a picture."

"Good," thought the boy and he waited for the teacher to tell him what to do. But the teacher didn't say anything. She just walked around the room. When she came to the boy she said, "Don't you want to make a picture?"

"Yes," said the boy. "What are we going to make?"

"Well, I don't know until you make it," said the teacher.

"How should I make it?" said the boy.

"Why, any way you like!"

BARRIERS TO CREATIVITY

"And any color?"

"Any color," said the teacher. "If everyone made the same thing in the same color, how would I know who made what and which was which?"

"I don't know," said the boy, and he began to draw a flower. It was red with a green stem.

WE'RE HELD BACK BY OUR FEARS

When I moved from the San Francisco Bay area out to Rocklin (20 miles east of Sacramento), I rented a U-haul truck. U-Haul trucks have a governor on them that prevents them from going over 55 miles per hour.

"The only thing we have to fear is fear itself."

FRANKLIN D. ROOSEVELT

Fear can be like a governor on our lives that prevents us from doing what we are capable of doing and drains our creativity and imagination. Consider this: What is the absolute worst thing that can happen to you? Death! So what if you die? All of us have to die sometime, and if you're a Christian, you know where you're going when you die. So, let's get over our fears of discovering and trying something new and different. We grow up too fast, we stop dreaming too early, and we develop the ability to worry at far too young an age.

One of the most effective ways to combat fear is to acknowledge it. When NASA studied the effects of space travel on humans, it noticed that some astronauts consistently suffered from motion or stress sickness, while others didn't. NASA deemed these reactions to be manifestations of fear, and concluded that the major difference between the two groups was that the second group had acknowledged in advance that they were going to be afraid, whereas the first group had not.

But acknowledging our fears does not mean we spend our days worrying. Mark Twain had keen insight into the minds of people who spend either too much time worrying about the future and past, or too much time dreaming up imaginary problems with terrifying consequences. He reminds us of the

unnecessary misery caused by worry: "I have lived through some pretty terrible things—some of which actually happened."

Fear can paralyze us and keep us from taking action. And often our fears are evoked by the anticipation of pain, danger, loss, or change—whether real or imagined. Let's take a closer look at few of the fears that are most debilitating:

Fear of failure

This fear is probably the most obvious. We're afraid we'll try something new, and it won't work. We might fail at it. It could be a total flop. If it's a big enough flop, we might even lose our jobs. So we don't even try.

Of course, you can also fail by continuing to do the same old thing. In fact, if what you've been doing has been less than successful, and you keep doing it, your failure is pretty much guaranteed! So why not try something new?

Even the best ideas can be stymied by our fear of failure. We can interrupt or shut down our creative juices if we're always checking to make sure there are no negative results. Often, we're like the little boy who planted an onion plant in his garden, and once the leaves came through the ground, he kept yanking the plant out of the ground to see if it was growing. Of course, it died. If we focus continually on how our efforts might be received, we can kill our creativity.

> "Courage is resistance to fear; mastery of fear, not absence of fear."
>
> MARK TWAIN

Fear of success

This might sound silly at first, but some people fear that if they come up with a creative idea or do something significant, then people will expect that level of creativity from them all of the time. They are afraid of the pressure that success might bring. Or they fear they might be known as "one-hit wonders." But would that be so bad? Would it be so bad if the only thing you came up with was White-Out or Barbie or the iPod or *The Purpose-Driven Life* or the Harry Potter series?

Fear of change

What's QWERTYUIOP? If you spend much time at a typewriter or computer, you probably know this pattern as the top row of letters on your keyboard. But think about this: If you were to design a computer or typewriter keyboard for the first time, today, what is the probability that you would arrange the keys in this manner? Not a chance—unless you're a masochist.

You might be surprised to learn that this familiar sequence of letters was not used on the first typewriters. In the 1870s Sholes and Co., a leading manufacturer of typewriters, was receiving complaints from customers that typewriter keys kept jamming and sticking together. In response—as an interim solution—the engineers rearranged the keys into an illogical sequence as a way of slowing typists down until a better solution could be found. For example, the letters "O" and "I" are the third and sixth most frequently used letters in the English language, yet the engineers positioned them so they required more movement and were depressed by weaker fingers. By the time engineers developed an improved design, typists had learned this sequence of keys and did not want the discomfort of "unlearning" again.

Today we have computers that can process keystrokes much faster than any human operator can type. Yet we are still using an irrational, unproductive system because that's the way we've always done it, and we don't want to learn something new.

Change is hard, and most of us avoid it when we can. The only people who like to be changed are babies—and they still cry most of the time!

The fear of change is especially destructive for those of us in ministry. We should do our best never to stifle the creativity that exists in every young person due to our own fear of change. Too many times we end up putting kids in a box and limiting what they can become, all in the name of conformity. Don't do this to your students! They are far too precious in God's eyes for us to destroy that wonderful spontaneity and love of life.

Instead we should seek to bring a spirit of creativity to everything we do in our youth groups—games, activities, meetings, talks, camps, Bible studies, worship, and every other aspect of our work with kids. By altering what we do, by giving new life to the old, we can get teenagers excited and involved in making the youth group their own, different from anyone else's.

But there's a problem we have to face. Fear of change isn't just inside us. It's all around us—especially in the church.

Not everybody welcomes creativity. Most churches are thrilled to have nice, predictable, comfortable youth groups where students are happily involved in the activities, growing in numbers, and satisfied with the programs. Youth workers are supposed to teach teenagers what to believe and how to act, so that when they are older, they will not depart from the faith. Most churches don't want risk. They don't want trouble. Most churches are quite happy to support creativity in the youth group...as long as it isn't too creative.

Creativity sounds like a nice idea that everyone can support. But when it meddles with our comfort level, when it disturbs our long-held beliefs, when it interferes with our worldviews or threatens our values, we're not too sure. Then creativity becomes scary.

Think about the way people reacted to Jesus. The religious leaders of his time had no real problem with him as long as he would stay in the Messiah box they had created, as long as he did what they thought a Messiah should do. As long as Jesus didn't break the rules, trample over the entrenched religious laws, or challenge their image of God, the religious leaders were happy to let him lead his merry band of followers.

But Jesus did break the rules. He confounded expectations. He was creative, inventive, and unpredictable. As a result he created enemies.

If you think the church has changed, and that the world is ready to welcome the kind of creativity Christ embodied, think again. Creativity threatens the status quo and disrupts those who are comfortable. Leonard Ravenhill once wrote, "If Jesus had preached the same message that ministers preach today, he would never have been crucified." But creativity also attracts the unattractive, reaches the unreachable, converts the unconverted, brings healing to the unhealable, and health to the unhealthy. And that's exactly what troubles most people.

THERE'S JUST NOT ENOUGH...

Our creativity can also be blocked by a "scarcity mentality" that believes we'll never have what we need to do what we can imagine. For example, we might think...

We don't have enough time.

This is not true. Everyone has the same amount of time. Bill Gates, Warren Buffett, Billy Graham, and Mother Teresa have (or had) the same time limitations you do: Everyone has 24 hours in a day, 7 days in a week, and 52 weeks in a year. It is not like some people have an extra hour tucked away somewhere that they can pull out in an emergency. It is not a matter of having more time, but of making the best use of the time we have.

Or maybe our concern is...

We don't have enough money.

As is the case with time, the real issue is how we use the money we have. In fact, lack of money can force us to be more creative and can often inspire even greater ideas. Walt Disney Company, Hewlett-Packard, and Apple all began in garages. Group Publishing began in a back room in the home of Thom Shultz's parents.

Mike Yaconelli and Wayne Rice began Youth Specialties out of the trunk of a car at a youth ministry conference in the mountains outside Los Angeles in 1969. They printed 100 copies of the first *Ideas* book on a mimeograph machine in Mike's church. They bought binders at a local stationary store, and Wayne silkscreened the book's cover.

So many great companies and ministries have done their most brilliant work in penny-pinching, cluttered, and even shabby surroundings. Most people in growing ministries spend very little time thinking about their surroundings. They have the best kind of tunnel vision: They are focused on what God can do in and through them.

But maybe the issue is...

We don't have enough knowledge.

In the movie *Bruce Almighty*, the character played by Jim Carey keeps asking God for a sign telling him what to do. The camera then shows us signs everywhere, but Jim fails to see them. The knowledge he needs is there, he just doesn't realize it. In the same way, we already have a lot of knowledge. The question is how we're using the knowledge we have creatively.

BAD ATTITUDES

Even if we get past concerns about whether we have adequate time, money, and knowledge, we can get tripped up by negative attitudes and assumptions. Let's talk about a few of the worst offenders:

"We've always done it this way."

Sometimes conventional wisdom and beliefs about what we've "always done" or "always thought" can be problematic. I encourage my students at the University to question age-old clichés. Consider the classic statements below. Are they really true? Is there another way to look at life?

- Curiosity killed the cat.

  - What does this say about curiosity? What do you think?

- Too many cooks spoil the broth.

  - What does this say about working as a team? What do you think?

- You can't teach an old dog new tricks.

  - What does this say about older dogs/people? What do you think?

- Beauty is only skin-deep.

  - What does this say about physically attractive people? What do you think?

- He who hesitates is lost.

  - What does this say about pausing and evaluating your situation? What do you think?

- Don't count your chickens before they're hatched.

  - What does this say about considering possibilities? What do you think?

- Better to have loved and lost than never to have loved at all.

  - What does this say about lost love? What do you think?

BARRIERS TO CREATIVITY

I'm not advocating you do anything that's illegal, immoral, or unethical as you challenge existing presuppositions. Nor am I encouraging anarchy or that we throw out everything you've always thought to be true. But I think it is healthy to periodically reexamine the principles we've accepted.

"To some, creativity is a sin. According to these folks, what was good enough for Paul should be good enough for us. They are suspicious of anything new and always worry that new means liberal. Throughout the Bible its God who constantly forces the religious people to recognize the newness of life, the fresh wind of the Holy Spirit. God used rocks, sticks, mud, water, furnaces, lions, fish, fire, earthquakes, wind, writing on a wall, donkeys, slingshots, perfume, snakes, wine, sheep, money, fig trees, wheat, seeds, pigs, frogs, locusts, and prostitutes. And we've just described the tip of the iceberg! Continually, God changed the types of people through whom he spoke and the ways in which his message was communicated. So when people believe God works only one way, they have bad theology. When God works, there is no limit to his creativity. God can communicate through anything or anyone."

MIKE YACONELLI, *THE CORE REALITIES OF YOUTH MINISTRY*

"Everyone has to be like us."

Theodor Seuss Geisel (aka Dr. Seuss) published more than 60 books for children before he died in 1991. Just before his death, he was working on a new book about an out-of-the-ordinary, unconventional school. His editor, Janet Schulman, received from Dr. Seuss's secretary 14 pages filled with penciled sketches and other information about where he planned to take the story. After holding on to these pages for a few years, Janet hired two other authors, Jack Prelutsky and Lane Smith, to finish the book, which was a celebration of individuality and creativity, and a questioning of the value of modern day standardized achievement tests (such as the PSAT, SAT, GMAT, LSAT, and MCAT to name a few). The book, *Hooray For Diffendoofer Day!*, was published in 1998. I highly recommend you read it.

In his book *Holy Wow*, Jeff White came up some wonderful questions to help us consider what the Diffendoofer School might have to teach our churches and ministries:

1. What kinds of subjects would a Diffendoofer church teach? Think of at least three.

2. What kinds of character traits would the leaders in a Diffendoofer church be known for? Do you think those traits would be suitable in a youth ministry? Why or why not?

3. Name some aspects (if any) of your youth ministry that might be more likely to be found in Flobbertown.

AWAKENING
YOUR CREATIVITY

4. What specific qualities make a Diffendoofer church different from a Flobbertown church? Name five.

5. In what ways could your youth ministry be more Diffendoofer-like? In what ways could it be less like Flobbertown?

Another example of the problem of expecting everyone to be just like us can be seen in an episode of *King of the Hill.* In this episode Hank Hill doesn't know what to do about the upseting behavior of his son, Bobby. A friend suggests Hank should get Bobby involved in a local church youth group. Re-membering his own experience at church as a child, Hank dresses Bobby up in a dark suit and tie with a white shirt and gives him a large black Bible to take to the youth group. When Bobby is dropped off in front of the church, he is not happy.

Bobby hears some noises behind the church and finds a bunch of kids skateboarding. When he realizes this is the youth group, he is thrilled. Soon Bobby has adopted the language and dress of those Christian skateboarders, and it's Hank's turn to be unhappy. This was not how Hank came to know God, nor how he expressed his thoughts about God when he was a teen.

Hank Hill is not alone. There are many parents and youth leaders who are trying to create spiritual clones of themselves rather than nurturing and supporting young people on their own unique spiritual paths. Everyone's spiritual journey is not going to be exactly the same.

"It'll never work."

Throughout my 40-plus years of ministry, I have gathered a large collection of examples of people throughout history who have been negative, pessimistic, and downright discouraging of others' ideas. I have listed just a few:

- In 1861 Phillip Reiss, a German, invented a machine that could broadcast music. He was also close to inventing a machine that could transmit speech. Every communication expert in Germany convinced him there was no market for such a device, as the telegraph was good enough. He discontinued his work and Alexander Graham Bell fifteen years later invented the telephone and became a multimillionaire, with Germany as his first, most eager client.

- In 1872 Pierra Pachet, professor of physiology at Toulouse University, said, "Louis Pasteur's theory of germs is ridiculous fiction."

- The King of Prussia predicted the failure of railroads because: "No one will pay good money to get from Berlin to Potsdam in one hour when he can ride his horse in one day for free."

- A London professor at the dawn of the railroad, when the top speed was 25 m.p.h., wrote: "Rail travel at high speed is not possible because passengers, unable to breathe, would die of asphyxia."

- In 1899 Charles Duell, the commissioner of the U.S. Patent Office, recommended that the government abolish the office because everything that could be invented had been invented.

- In 1903 a banker advised against investing in Ford Motor Company because: "The horse is here to stay, but the automobile is only a novelty, a fad."

- In 1905 Grover Cleveland said: "Sensible and responsible women do not want to vote."

- In 1938 Chester Carlson invented xerography. Practically every major corporation, including IBM and Kodak, scoffed at his idea and turned him down. They claimed that no one in their right mind would buy an expensive copier when carbon paper was so cheap and plentiful.

- In 1943 Thomas Watson, chairman of IBM said: "I think there is a world market for maybe five computers."

- A famous movie studio head, commenting on the future of TV, said, "People will soon get tired of staring at a plywood box every night."

- In 1955 Variety magazine's assessment of rock and roll was "It will be gone by June."

- In 1977 Ken Olson, president, chairman and founder of Digital Equipment Corp., said, "There is no reason anyone would want a computer in their home."

- Fred Smith, while a student at Yale, came up with the concept of Federal Express, a national overnight delivery service. The U.S. Postal Service, UPS, his own business professor, and virtually every delivery expert in the United States predicted his venture would fail. Based on their experiences in the industry, no one, they said, would pay more money for speed and reliability.

My point in sharing all these examples is simple: Don't let people like this get to you. Don't let them pull you down and discourage you about coming up with new ideas and fresh thinking. You will always have critics. As teacher and author Howard Hendricks would often say, "Where there is light, there will be bugs."

It's equally important not to be dismissive of others' creative ideas. Here's a list of phrases that are almost guaranteed to shut down every new or innovative idea. Next time you want to stifle all creativity in a planning session, try responding to your team with one or more of these phrases:

- We tried that before.
- We're all too busy to do that.
- That change is too radical.
- That's not practical.
- We've never done that before.
- Christians don't do that.
- Let's get back to reality.
- Why change? The old way works fine.
- You're right, but…
- We're not ready for that.
- We don't have the authority/time/money/equipment/space/personnel.
- It isn't in the budget.
- Let's give it more thought.
- That's what liberals (or conservatives) do.
- Where'd you dig up that idea?
- We did all right without it.
- Our parents/denomination/church leaders/congregation won't like it.
- It can't be done.
- It's too inconvenient.
- I know a church that tried that and it didn't work.

BARRIERS TO CREATIVITY

But even if you find yourself expressing these kinds of sentiments, there's hope. Ezekiel 37:1-14 tells us God can breathe new life into dead bones. We have no limitations and nothing to fear because we have God's support: "I can do everything through Christ, who gives me strength" (Philippians 4:13, NLT). In fact, Romans tells us that Jesus has already helped us succeed: "In all these things we are more than conquerors through him who loved us" (Romans 8:37). We've been filled with the strength of the very God who created creativity so we can shout, "YES! Of course we can!"

SO-NOT-DONE QUESTIONS

If you haven't already done so, track down and read a copy of Dr. Seuss's *Hooray for Diffendoofer Day!* and then tackle the questions raised by Jeff White on pages 32 and 33. Then consider the questions below:

1. Take the problem or opportunity you've been working on and consider how a 10-year-old might view it. What questions would a 10-year-old ask?

2. How long has it been since you've taken 15 minutes to walk 20 feet?

3. How do some churches stifle creativity?

4. What fears do you have about trying something new?

5. Have you ever tried to turn your students into spiritual clones of yourself rather than encouraging them to become all God created them to be?

STUPIDITY, SACRED COWS, AND HOLY ENTHUSIASM

CHAPTER THREE

If we're going to be creative in ministry, we need to take a few risks. We all know people who choose safety and security to such an extreme that they imprison themselves and profoundly limit their life experiences. But sometimes our attempts to be innovative and electrifying can go too far, crossing the line from creative to just plain dumb. Even though it can sometimes seem like a very fine line, it's important to find the right balance...

> ...between freedom and security

> ...between risk and safety

> ...between courage and recklessness

> ...between creativity and foolishness.

This is especially true as we try to bring greater creativity to our work with students. Sometimes finding the right balance can be a real challenge.

For example, consider the youth minister who came to a new position years ago and was eager to bond with his students. He purchased two dozen eggs, and then took four of the high school boys for a drive in downtown Atlanta, encouraging them to throw the eggs at pedestrians. He was arrested and lost his job within a month. Stupid!

Or how about the youth leader who was driving a van full of junior high boys on a cross-country trip? Along the way they started making silly bets that grew more and more ridiculous. Eventually the boys and their youth leader made a bet that would

require the loser of the bet to strip down to his underpants and remain that way until they stopped to fill the van with gas. The youth leader won the bet, so the 12 young boys removed everything but their underwear, while the clothed male adult youth leader continued driving the van down the highway. They were all laughing so hard that the youth leader didn't notice how his speed had increased until he saw the flashing red lights on the police car behind him. Stupid!

Let me tell you about a stupid blunder I made during my early years in youth ministry. I had just arrived as the part-time youth worker at a church in southern California. Noticing that the youth room was painted a dingy, hospital-white color, I suggested to the kids that they paint the room.

I rounded up cans of donated paint and met the kids at 7 a.m. the next Saturday. When the kids couldn't agree what color to paint the room, they decided on a "creative compromise." They would paint each of the four walls a different color. After we painted one wall white, another black, and the last two blue and red, my students and I cleaned up and went out for breakfast. Mission accomplished.

There was just one problem: I didn't realize that another group met in that room on Sunday mornings while the youth group was at the first worship service. The other group was the senior citizens.

During the first worship service, I sat at the front of the church, beaming. I felt proud of the work my students had accomplished—until the senior pastor slid into the chair next to me and told me the senior citizens were really upset. "You can kiss your job good-bye," he whispered. "I can't save you. You're dead meat."

> "There's a fine line between genius and insanity. I have erased that line."
>
> —OSCAR LEVANT

> "There is a fool in each of us, you know. A rash, brash, harebrained, audacious, imprudent, ill-suited, spontaneous, impolitic, daredevil fool, which, in most of us, was long ago hog-tied and locked in the basement. If you want to see a full-fledged fool in action, watch an undisciplined child. (The more undisciplined, the better!) Oblivious to concepts of appropriate behavior, driven by rampant curiosity and innocent lust. Raw genius. Resolutely stumbling into hurt and wondrous discovery. Inspired, annoying, rapturous, petulant."
>
> GORDON RAY MACKENZIE, *ORBITING THE GIANT HAIRBALL*

AWAKENING YOUR CREATIVITY

I sheepishly left the worship service and immediately went to the senior citizens' class. I thought it was a bold move, given the circumstances. I entered the room and, before they could say anything, asked if they'd noticed the room had been painted. They had. I then told them how excited I was to work in a church where the high schoolers were so spiritual.

I then quickly explained that the wall on the left was blue to symbolize heaven. The wall behind them was black, which stood for sin, and pointed out how we'd positioned the chairs so they were facing away from that wall. The wall in front of them was white, which stood for purity. And the red wall on the right symbolized the blood of Christ.

> "The Electrolux Vacuum Cleaner Company, a privately held corporation in Finland, was trying to break into the North American market. They had plenty of English speakers on staff, but no Americans. Their lead marketing slogan? *If it sucks, it must be an Electrolux.*"
>
> JOHN MEDINA, *BRAIN RULES*

What could they say? Those colors remained in that room for the next 14 years, long after I had left the church. No one could paint over the blood of Jesus.

Now, I am not advocating that a youth worker lie to a roomful of seniors. Youth workers can be an impulsive group. Sometimes you have to take advantage of opportunities and keep up with the kids. But with hindsight I should have asked permission. I should have checked it out with someone over me. But I didn't. Stupid!

Ministry doesn't happen without taking risks. But they should be prudent risks, calculated risks. Failing is acceptable, as long as it doesn't become a habit. There are limits to how many errors a ministry can absorb. In the same way that the three key words in real estate are *location*, *location*, and *location*, with creative ideas, it's often all about *timing*, *timing*, and *timing*.

VALUE TRADITION BUT BEWARE OF SACRED COWS

I miss TV theme songs. We don't have as many anymore—or at least they're not as memorable. Those little tunes would work their way into your head and settle there for a lifetime. They were used to introduce characters, establish plots, or set a program's mood and tone.

See if you can match these lyrics with the TV series each song introduced:

THEME SONG:

- Come listen to a story 'bout a man named Jed
- They're creepy and they're kooky, mysterious and spooky
- Overture, curtains, lights, this is it, the night of nights
- You're gonna make it after all
- Just sit right back and you'll hear a tale, a tale of a fateful trip
- Here's the story, of a lovely lady, who was bringing up three very lovely girls
- The chores...The stores...Fresh air...Times Square
- Welcome back, your dreams were your ticket out
- Where everybody knows your name
- Oh yeah, we're moving on up, to the East Side
- They're the modern Stone Age family. From the town of Bedrock, they're a page right out of history.
- I'll be there for you
- Whenever he gets in a fix, he reaches into his bag of tricks

TV SERIES:

- *The Mary Tyler Moore Show*
- *Friends*
- *Looney Tunes*
- *Green Acres*
- *The Flintstones*
- *Felix the Cat*
- *The Jeffersons*
- *The Beverly Hillbillies*
- *The Addams Family*
- *Cheers*
- *Gilligan's Island*
- *Welcome Back Kotter*
- *The Brady Bunch*

Today's television producers don't use theme songs the same way. They believe today's audience needs something different. Maybe they're right— but I miss those traditional theme songs.

One of the most famous songs in the musical *Fiddler on the Roof* celebrates the importance and value of tradition. I couldn't agree more. We must appreciate the past and what has gone on before us, especially in the church. There is a great value in knowing our past and cherishing many of the traditions in a ministry.

But sometimes there are "sacred cows" in our ministries that need to be overhauled. As the old saying goes, "Sacred cows make great steaks." There are times when passionate ministries have to be willing to slaughter some sacred cows. I am talking about parts of the ministry that are no longer effective or aren't reaching kids or have outlived their usefulness.

It's been said that one definition of *insanity* is "doing the same thing we did yesterday, but hoping for a different result today." We all know most churches have some sacred cows, but even our youth ministries can be full of sacred cows. Maybe it's time to grill up some of those holy heifers!

Here are just a few "youth ministry sacred cows" I've discovered while giving seminars to youth pastors around the country. I hope these examples will get you started thinking about some of the traditional "sacred cows" in your own ministry:

- Curriculum you must use at this church

- Camps you must attend

- Rooms you can and cannot use

- Times and locations we always have for meetings

- Yearly programs we always have

Periodically, you need to inspect your entire ministry and ask if the various programs and approaches you're using remain effective. Ask yourself, "Why did this program, concept, project, or idea come to be?" Then follow this question with, "Do these reasons still exist?" and "Does this program still address the need effectively?" If the answer to either question is "no," it's time to rethink that strategy—and maybe even time to eliminate it entirely.

Before we move on, let me share one related idea that's become an essential part of my ministry philosophy: No matter how creative or exciting a new idea might be, I need to figure out which of my current responsibilities I will let go of before taking on something new. Like most other youth pastors, my plate is already full. So before I add another project or responsibility, either I need to hand off responsibility for something I'm currently doing, or I have to ask, "What old thing needs to go to make room for something new?"

NOT AGE BUT ATTITUDE

Consider the following newspaper headline from a few years ago: "Oldest U.S. Worker, at 102, Says His Job Still a 'Pleasure.'" The story is told of Milton Garland, who had worked for the Frick Company of Waynesboro, Pennsylvania, for 78 years! "'I love the work I am doing," Frick said.

The same attitude can also be seen at nearly the opposite end of the age spectrum. Richard Barton, who founded the online travel service Microsoft Expedia when he was in his early twenties, once said this about his own job: "Work is not work. It's a hobby that you happen to get paid for."

> "I highly recommend reading books written by great men and women of the past and not just the new, popular books with the latest thoughts. The reason I recommend reading the older books is not that they had it all together. They had their own blind spots as we have ours. The difference is that they did not have the same blind spots."
>
> C.S. LEWIS

Wayne Dennis once studied the lives of 738 creative scientists and concluded that age does not inhibit creativity. Dennis's research included scholars and artists who were still working creatively at ages up to 79. Dennis suggested that youthful vigor did not seem to play a major role in creativity. It seems that age doesn't really matter unless you are cheese.

Michelangelo worked on the architectural design for the dome of St. Peter's Basilica from age 72 to 88; French actress Sarah Bernhardt lost a leg while in her early 70s, but continued to perform on stage until her death at age 78; Architect Frank Lloyd Wright completed his design of New York's Guggenheim Museum at age 91; and Agatha Christie oversaw production of her film *Murder on the Orient Express* at age 84. These examples clearly demonstrative that people can stay creative well into old age.

When I was speaking at a Youth Specialties convention in Atlanta several years ago, I interviewed Evelyn McClusky, founder of the Miracle Book Club. I wanted to speak with Evelyn because, at age 104, she was the oldest living youth leader in the world. What a joy to speak with that amazing woman! When I interviewed her, she was still going strong with the aid of a walker—and the woman who was taking care of Evelyn was 75 years old! Evelyn's mind was humming along; she was sharp as a tack. It was hard to get a sound bite from her about her life because all she wanted to talk about was Jesus. How cool is that?

> "Life is not measured by the number of breaths we take, but by the number of moments that take our breath away."
>
> ANONYMOUS

Back in the 1940s Evelyn had started a Bible-study meeting for teens. When I asked her why she decided to call the group "The Miracle Book Club," she said it was because the kids she was trying to reach would not attend if she called it a Bible study. At its peak there were 1,000 Miracle Book Clubs all over the United States, most of them staffed by women. The founders of both Young Life and Youth for Christ were part of these clubs when they were students.

Evelyn's ministry was built on the idea of turning any conversation to Jesus. I asked that day what her goals were. She said she wanted to finish writing her twentieth book and then die. That's exactly what she did. She died at age 106.

If there's ever a youth ministry hall of fame this side of heaven, Henrietta Mears is another hero of the faith who belongs there. Henrietta was a large woman with thick glasses, dressed in red, and wore flamboyant hats and multiple rings. She began working with junior highers when she was a student at the University of Minnesota. She later became the educational director at Hollywood Presbyterian Church. Even at an old age, she led a Sunday Bible study with 500 college students. She was passionate and engaging as she spoke.

Henrietta mentored Dick Halverson, who became chaplain of the U.S. Senate. She was an adviser to Bill and Vonette Bright, founders of Campus Crusade. She had a primary influence on the life of Bob Munger, one of my professors at Fuller Theological Seminary and author of the very popular booklet *My Heart, Christ's Home.* As a young Sunday School teacher, Henrietta thought the available curriculum of her day was unappealing, so she wrote

I will never forget the first time I spoke in a church service. I'd become a Christian at age 16 and had done a little street preaching on Sunset Strip in Hollywood, but I'd never spoken in a church. The Christian college I attended sent students out to speak at neighborhood churches on Sunday evenings. The first time I was asked to do this, I was extremely nervous. A girl from the college came with me to do special music.

There were 15 or 20 people in attendance that hot September night. They started the service by singing a hymn I disliked, "Beulah Land." (I never could understand why I'd want to go to a place called Beulah Land, and some of the words seemed so negative, such as "in God's Word we are retreating.") By the end of the hymn, I was starting to perspire.

The other student from the college got up to sing her special music. She was nervous, too. She got her heal caught in an old metal floor heater in the center aisle and fell on her posterior, crushing not only her dress but her pride. But she got back up and through her song—and then it was time for me to speak.

I was scared to death. In the pew right in front of me sat a little gray-haired man. (He looked a lot like I do now!) As I got up to speak, I grabbed the back of that pew, not realizing it wasn't fastened down. The pew flipped over, dumping the man on the floor. I picked him up and dusted him off, apologizing profusely, and made my way to the stage.

I'd worked on four different sermon outlines and finally decided to go with a message about the apostle Peter. I talk fast, even when I am calm—and I definitely wasn't calm that evening. I went through my entire "Peter message" in three minutes. That seemed too short, so I started speaking from my second outline. Eleven minutes later, I'd clipped through all four of my message outlines. When I finished speaking, I wanted to crawl out of the building. I concluded that God would make better use of me as an assistant manager at a gas station.

On the way out, an older lady grabbed my arm. I was prepared for the worst. Looking me in the eye she said, "Son, that was tremendous! Why, that was better than the apostle Paul would have done."

Anyone with half a brain cell could have listed 400 things wrong with what I'd done that night. But this woman was so encouraging that I walked out of that church thinking, "Billy Graham, move over. Here I come!"

her own and, in 1933, founded Gospel Light Publishing. Six years later she established Forrest Home Christian Conference Center. She died in the late 1960s. Billy Graham spoke at her funeral and commented that, except for his mother and his wife, no other woman had a greater influence on his life, adding, "She is one of the greatest Christians I have ever known."

People can continue to be creative after becoming senior citizens. It is true that our brains lose cells as we age, but our bodies compensate, as new brain cells are born continually well into old age. Although an aging circulatory system can reduce the blood supply that brings oxygen and glucose to your brain, regular exercise that elevates the heart rate can help you maintain your cognitive abilities later in life. Even if you are older and have never exercised before, studies show that you can dramatically improve your circulation in just a few months.

PASSIONATE ENTHUSIASM

IQ tests alone do not accurately predict who will be creative. Creative people focus on finding the right problems, not just the right answers. Yale University's Robert Sternberg, well known in the field of creativity, maintains that IQ plays less of a role in creativity and other important aspects of life than do things like personality, experience, and socioeconomic factors. Many studies have shown that the most intelligent people are not always the most creative.

Motivation and drive are also an important part of creativity. A motivated person will keep looking for alternatives and new possibilities when everyone else is satisfied with the obvious option. Motivation can mean spending five hours a week trying to find a better way of doing something, when others are spending only five minutes.

The most effective motivation is intrinsic—it comes form the inside. If intrinsic motivation is high, if we are passionate about what we are doing, creativity will flow. Internally motivated people seem fired up, stimulated, animated, electrified, and galvanized. External expectations and rewards can kill intrinsic motivation and thus kill creativity. When intrinsic motivation drops off, so does our willingness to explore new avenues and different ideas.

Creative people have a burning passion that drives them to accomplish the seemingly impossible no matter the age. They are enthusiastic. The Greek word *enthousiasmos* means "God within you." If you are a Christian, God is within you; therefore, you cannot help but be enthusiastic about your mission in life.

The most effective way to tap the creativity of the people who partner with us in ministry is to encourage their passion for the task at hand. Creativity,

Enthusiasm is contagious. Many years ago I was flying from Los Angeles to Cincinnati by way of Dallas. As we boarded the plane, I noticed about 16 women scattered throughout the plane, all wearing red-white-and-blue straw hats. One of these women took a seat next to me. I thought the hats were a bit unusual, but soon forgot them—'til the gal next to me got up and walked to the front of the capacity-filled plane.

She turned to faced all the passengers and said, "Ladies are we ready?" Suddenly, these women began to sing "I've got the Mary Kay enthusiasm down in my heart..." I was bewildered!

Then the leader said to everyone, "Put down your drinks." A gray-haired 55-year-old businessman on the other side of me put down his drink. I cracked up! Then the Mary Kay leader got the whole plane clapping as the gals sang this little song.

When she finally sat down, I was dumbfounded. But for the rest of that flight, I kept thinking: If these women are that enthusiastic about Mary Kay Cosmetics, how much more enthusiastic should I be about working with God's kids?

passion, and enthusiasm all thrive in an atmosphere of optimism and confidence in the future.

The book of Acts shows how enthusiastic the early Christians were. For example: "We cannot stop telling about the wonderful things we saw Jesus do and heard him say" (Acts 4:20, TLB). I hope you thank God every day that he has allowed you to be a youth leader. I know there are days when you feel like you want to throw in the towel. But remember, youth work is not a 100-yard dash. It is a 26-mile marathon. And remember these words from the apostle Paul: "Do you not know that in a race all the runners run, but only one gets the prize? Run in such a way as to get the prize" (1 Corinthians 9:24).

SO-NOT-DONE QUESTIONS

1. What things have you said or done that "crossed the line" from creative to foolish or reckless?

2. What sacred cows in your church and ministry have outlived their usefulness? What can you do about that?

3. What are you willing to handoff or drop before creating something new?

4. How old is too old for youth ministry?

5. How do you sense God working in you?

6. Describe an older person who is still going strong with a love for God and kids and is still looking for creative ideas on how to reach and minister to them. What can you learn from that person?

7. What gets you excited? What turns you on?

8. Are you enthusiastic about your ministry? Why—or why not?

AWAKENING YOUR CREATIVITY

TEN QUALITIES OF CREATIVE YOUTH LEADERS

CHAPTER FOUR

I believe God longs to touch your student ministry so that your work with youth is continually growing to reflect the image of Jesus more completely. No matter how great your youth ministry is today—no matter how good your programs, strategies, and responding skills, no matter how deep and genuine your community—there is always room for growth and change. God desires not only to change us into the people he created us to be, but also to change our ministries from what they are today into what he intends them to be. Here are just a few of the ways I believe God wants our ministries to be transformed...

FROM:	TO:
Getting kids to come to church	Getting kids to be the church
Focusing on entertainment	Focusing on empowering and equipping
Adult volunteers as chaperones	Adult volunteers as shepherds
Student leaders as observers	Student leaders as co-ministers
Structure found in calendar	Structure found in community
Success measured in numbers	Success measured in depth

Source: *Youth Specialties CORE Seminar Notebook, 2008*

But for our ministries to become what God desires, we must be open to change. Our ministries must say YES! to God's transforming Spirit. John 3:8 tells us God's spirit is like the wind which "blows wherever it pleases." You cannot put God in a box. You cannot put creative people in a box, either.

Creative youth ministries will require leaders who are risk-taking, failure-willing, exploration-minded models of God's creative spark. Creative youth ministries will foster and cherish childlike wonder. These ministries make room for the unique and odd. Most creative kids are often a bit odd; they don't find a place in youth ministries that are committed to conformity. While kids who all follow their own compass can sometimes drive their youth ministers crazy, such kids can also push their youth ministries to serve God in new ways we might never discover on our own.

In this chapter I am describing qualities I've found in the most creative youth leaders and their ministries. My goal is not to make you feel guilty if you feel you lack some of these qualities but to encourage you to find ways to awaken these qualities and characteristics in your life and ministry. And if you are fortunate to have these qualities, I hope this chapter will help you find new and better ways to use them to help your ministry become everything God wants it to be.

The theme song for television's *CSI* comes from the classic rock group, The Who. The opening music raises the question, "Who are you?" and the question is repeated throughout the song:

Who are you?

Who, who, who, who?

Who are you?

Who, who, who, who?

A creative youth leader knows who she is. A creative youth leader knows the lens through which she views the world. Creative youth leaders have a good understanding of their strengths, their weaknesses, and what really makes them tick.

In the early twentieth century, psychologist Carl Jung discovered that people had certain preferences in their thinking styles. For example, Jung observed that...

- Some people are *intuitive*, others are more *sensing*.

- Some rely primarily on *thinking*; others rely on *feeling*.

- Some are *extroverted*; others are *introverted*.

You're probably familiar with these terms if you've ever taken the Myers-Briggs test—a personality assessment developed by later researchers building on Jung's work. If you are not familiar with this evaluation tool, I'd encourage you to check it out. Knowing where you fall on these continuums can give you a better sense of who you are and help you be more effective in ministry.

But it's important not only to know who you are but also to know who your students and adults leaders are. Next time you get with your staff or students, try asking the group members what animal best describes them and then go around the room and have people explain why they chose a particular animal.

It's also essential to know the purpose of your ministry. One of the most important questions for any youth pastor to ask is: "What is the business of my

TEN QUALITIES OF CREATIVE YOUTH LEADERS

youth ministry?" It may seem like a simple question at first, but it's actually a difficult question. Think about it: Why does your ministry exist?

Bell Telephone, the first telephone company in the United States, wrestled with this question more than 100 years ago. And it surely seemed like a silly question to some folks. What could be more obvious than the telephone business in the late 1800s? But Theodore Vail was fired by the company back in 1890 when he dared to ask top management, "What is our business?" He was called back a decade later, when the consequences of the lack of an answer had become evident. Bell System, operating without a clear definition, had drifted into a severe crisis and was being threatened by a government takeover. Theodore Vail's answer was: "Our business is service, not telephones." That answer brought about radical innovations in Bell Telephone's business policy. It meant employee training and advertising that stressed service.

Fred Smith, founder of Federal Express, developed a successful company because he understood the essence of his business. He described it as delivering peace of mind, not just the transportation of goods.

If you want to infuse your work with students to be more creative and vital, it's essential to know who you are what your ministry is all about.

SO-NOT-DONE QUESTIONS

1. What comes closest to describing you in general and why?

    At home:

    • Key or lock?   • Pen or pencil?

    At work or school:

    • Microscope or telescope?   • Sitcom or drama?

    At church:

    • Text message or handwritten letter?   • Violin or tuba?

    At being creative:

    • Bicycle or scooter?   • Knife or fork?

2. How would you describe your ministry? What is its purpose? Why does your ministry exist?

AWAKENING YOUR CREATIVITY

Do you believe one plus one can be greater than two? When people combine their gifts and abilities, the end product can be more than just the sum of their individual efforts. Each person has his or her own worth and value. But when people are brought together and empowered to use their God-given gifts, it is almost mystical. When people work together, support one another, and create from one another's ideas, the end product is greater—more creative, more effective—than any of them could have produced alone. It seems to defy explanation, but the whole is somehow greater than the sum of its parts.

> "The Lone Ranger, the incarnation of the individual problem solver, is dead."
>
> WARREN BENNIS, *ORGANIZING GENIUS*

Xerox's Palo Alto Research Center (PARC) has birthed an enormous number of creative ideas. One of PARC's more unusual efforts is its Artist-in-Residence program, which pairs an artist with a computer scientist. These pairings have yielded some unusual multimedia technologies that may not have been conceived by computer scientists alone.

> "Plans fail for lack of counsel, but with many advisors they succeed."
>
> PROVERBS 15:22

Or consider the success of Tommy Hilfiger. How did an older white man from Connecticut who designs prep-school clothes spend years as one of the most popular designers in urban black America? Well, he filled his design team with diverse people—hip-hop performers and skateboarders and graffiti artists and others from a wide range of cultural and ethnic backgrounds.

When Jerry Hirshberg first set up the Nissan Design International studios in San Diego, he challenged himself to design the organization for creativity. He resisted the temptation to select only people whose gifts matched his own—highly intuitive, big-picture, visually oriented, right-brained thinkers. Instead, he also deliberately hired a few left-brained individuals who sought structure and always questioned "why" before proceeding. Initially, these individuals annoyed him; they seemed to be "anticreative" and threatened

TEN QUALITIES OF CREATIVE YOUTH LEADERS

by novelty. However, he soon came to realize that they simply came to the table with a different set of preparations and expectations.

> "The Medicis were a banking family in Florence in the 15th century who funded creators from a wide range of disciplines. Thanks to this family and a few others like it, sculptors, scientists, poets, philosophers, financiers, painters, and architects converged upon the city of Florence. There they found each other, learned from one another, and broke down barriers between disciplines and cultures. Together they forged a new world based on new ideas—what became known as the Renaissance. As a result, the city became the epicenter of a creative explosion, one of the most innovative eras in history. The effects of the Medici family can be felt even to this day."
>
> FRANS JOHANSSON, *THE MEDICI EFFECT*

The message for us in ministry is to recruit and welcome the contributions of people who are not like us. There are many types of diversity: Economic, generational, racial-ethnic, gender, and theological are just a few. Our ministries will be strengthened as we bring in new people, ideas, and concepts with which we are unfamiliar. We must be intentional in developing a community where diversity is not just tolerated but valued and celebrated.

Of course, simply recruiting people who are different from the norm for your group does not, in itself, guarantee creative output—especially if you're adding people who just look different. And the goal is not to pull in people whose different perspectives will simply irritate present group members and cause conflict. But welcoming diversity can have a powerful impact on your youth ministry team. It can help you reach students in ways you might never imagined yourself. It can open up a fresh new ways of looking at everyday activities.

Collaboration continually takes place in the arts. A classic example is Michelangelo's masterpiece, the ceiling of the Sistine Chapel. In our mind's eye, we imagine Michelangelo, looking remarkably like Charlton Heston, laboring alone on the scaffolding high above the chapel floor. But historian William E. Wallace says that 13 people collaborated with Michelangelo on the Sistine Chapel.

Geese are another great example of teamwork and collaboration. Next time you see geese flying along in V formation, consider what science has discovered about why they fly that way, and what it can teach us about teamwork. When geese fly together, as each bird flaps its wings, it creates uplift for the bird immediately following. By flying in V formation, the whole flock adds at least 71 percent greater flying range than if each bird flew on its own. The geese save energy and get where they are going more quickly and easily because they are traveling on the thrust of one another—similar

to race cars drafting behind each other. When a goose falls out of formation, it feels the drag and resistance of trying to go it alone—and quickly gets back into formation to take advantage of the lifting power of the bird in front. If we have as much sense as a goose, we will journey along with other people headed in the same direction.

When the lead goose in the V gets tired, it rotates back and another goose takes the lead. It is sensible to take turns doing demanding jobs, whether we're talking about people working in a ministry or geese flying south. And just as geese honk from behind to encourage those up front, we should encourage our leaders.

If a goose becomes too exhausted or ill and has to drop out of the flock, that bird is not abandoned. One or two stronger members will follow the failing goose to its resting place and will wait until the fallen goose is well enough to fly again or dies. Only then do they launch out on their own, or with another formation, to catch up with their group.

> "Monet and Renoir painted at times next to each other in the Barbizon woods. Their pieces of art were so similar that Monet had to look at the signature to tell if it was his or Renoir's. Braque and Picasso also had an intense creative collaboration, which gave birth to Cubism. For several years, they saw each other almost every day, talked constantly about their revolutionary new style, and painted as similarly as possible. They even dressed alike, in mechanics' clothes, and playfully compared themselves to the equally pioneering Wright brothers (Picasso called Braque, Wilbourg). Braque later described their creative interdependence as that of 'two mountaineers roped together.'"
>
> WARREN BENNIS, *ORGANIZING GENIUS*

Another way to combine talent is to elicit advice and information about your ministry from people who work in different fields. Get feedback about your ideas from many people. Different people can help you modify and improve the initial idea. Artist Leonardo da Vinci met and worked with the political theorist Niccolò Machiavelli on several projects, including using the diversion of a river as a weapon of war. William Shockley's invention of the transistor was a remarkable act of creativity, but it was made possibly only by his joint work with two others, Walter Brattain and John Bardeen. In music, I think of the way that songwriting duos like John Lennon and Paul McCarthy or Elton John and Bernie Taupin rose to heights that might never have been reached if these individuals worked alone.

To realize his vision of the first ever full-length animated feature film, Walt Disney assembled a great team of diverse talents. The result was his breakthrough film *Snow White and the Seven Dwarfs*. It was Disney's ability

Gordon MacKenzie tells this story about a waterskiing trip with his boss:

"My last boss at Hallmark, a fellow by the name of Bob Kipp, sat at the wheel of one of the corporate speedboats. I was at the end of a towline on water skis. We spent our time together skimming across great Lake Hallmark. Kipp was so sure of who he was, and why he was where he was, and where the power was, that he was not threatened at all when I would ski around in a wide arc until I was up even with the boat and sometimes even past it. He knew I was not going to start pulling the boat with him in it. It just doesn't work that way. The power remains in the boat. But, in allowing me to ski past him—in a sense, allowing me to lead— he would unleash in me an excitement about our enterprise that served our shared goals well."

GORDON RAY MACKENZIE, *ORBITING THE GIANT HAIRBALL*

to include people with a wide range of gifts and backgrounds, allowing each individual to retain his individuality while combining with others, that created the cooperative synthesis that made Disney's vision a reality.

There is great value in having a variety of people on your team because interacting with diverse people often gives us mental momentum. Think of a rocket just beginning to rise from its launching pad. It is at takeoff that the greatest energy is required. It's the same way in ministry and all other creative efforts. Getting an idea off the launching pad requires the most effort. Usually a group of diverse people can deliver the momentum better than one person striving alone.

SO-NOT-DONE QUESTIONS

1. Do you believe that one plus one can be greater than two when it comes to teams?

2. When has your team experienced synergy? How might you facilitate greater synergy in your ministry?

3. How diverse is your ministry team? How could you incorporate greater diversity?

4. How is your team similar to—or different from—geese in a V formation? Do you ever allow others to get out in front and lead?

5. Ask three to five people who work in other professions for their ideas about your problem or opportunity. Ask your child's school teacher, your neighbor, the waitress at your favorite restaurant, your mechanic, and your accountant. Describe the problem or opportunity you're facing and ask these people how they would approach it.

3 CREATIVE YOUTH LEADERS BRING DIVERSE PEOPLE TOGETHER AND WELCOME THE GIFTS OF ALL.

Youth leaders must be adept at the art of questioning. Questions help you estimate your challenges and provide conscious direction to your thinking. Asking questions of others solicits their input and opinions. And when you ask yourself a question, you force yourself to frame an issue and think about a solution.

The biggest mistake many of us make when leading discussions is asking too many of what psychologist H. Stephen Glen calls "closed questions." Closed questions can be answered with one word—which tends to limit discussion. Open questions, on the other hand, draw out a fuller response.

Young children are commonly asked closed questions: "How was school today?" "Did you have fun?" These can be answered with a yes or a no, a grunt or a shrug. When we ask closed questions, we say to them in effect, "I will reduce you to a carefully controlled response by limiting my exposure to your thoughts and ideas."

Instead of asking yes-no questions, we should ask open-ended questions like, "What kind of things happened to you today?" That type of question—followed by interested listening—will result in dialogue.

I still enjoy watching reruns of the old crime-investigation show *Columbo*—even though I've seen most of the episodes and usually know how things turn out. Columbo is a detective played by Peter Falk. He's unique in that he does not solve crimes primarily by looking for clues. He solves them by asking questions—and lots of them.

If we really want our questions to draw people's responses, it's important to think through the wording carefully. A few years back, a leading car manufacturer asked its employees for ideas on how the company could become more productive. They received few suggestions. They later reworded the question to ask, "How can you make your job easier?" They were inundated with ideas.

One of the most valuable medical discoveries of all time came about when Edward Jenner began asking a different question than had been asked be-

fore. Rather than continuing to ask why people were getting smallpox, Jenner asked why dairy workers seemed to never get the disease. From that question came the vaccination and the end of smallpox in the Western world.

Different questions bring new ways of looking at the same old problem. If you have ever taken the time to look at the wheels on a train you'll see they are flanged—meaning they have a lip that prevents the train from sliding off the track. Originally train wheels were not flanged; instead, the railroad tracks were. This came about because railroad safety experts had framed the question as, "How can tracks be made safer?" After producing hundreds of thousands of miles of expensive track with an unnecessary steep lip, the problem was redefined with a new question, "How can train wheels be made to stay on the track more securely?" The result was the flanged wheel—a much less expensive solution.

A simply way to change your question is by substituting a different verb. For example, if you're focused on increasing attendance at youth activities, you may want to ask the following questions:

- How can we attract students?
- How can we disciple students?
- How can we retain students?
- How can we bring back students?
- How can we target students?
- How can we inspire students?
- How can we encourage students?
- How can we acquire students?
- How can we spotlight students?
- How can we motivate students?

These questions are all interrelated—but each of them can cast a some-what different light on the same situation.

The Central Intelligence Agency had developed a series of questions to encourage agents to look at a challenge from many different angles. Here's just a sampling of the questions the CIA uses when considering a problem—and evaluating a potential solution:

- Why is it necessary to solve the problem?

- What benefits will you gain by solving the problem?

- What information do you have? Is the information sufficient? Redundant? Contradictory?

- What isn't the problem?

- Should you draw a diagram of the problem? A figure?

- Where are the boundaries of the problem?

- What are the constants (things that can't be changed) of the problem?

- Can you separate the various parts of the problem? Can you write them down? What are the relationships of the parts of the problem?

- Have you seen this problem before or in a slightly different form?

- Can you restate your problem? More generally? More specifically?

- What are the best, worst, and most probable cases you can imagine?

Here's a second sampling of questions used in considering any plan or proposed solution:

- Can you solve the whole problem? Part of the problem?

- What would you like the resolution to be? Can you picture it?

- Can you separate the steps in the problem-solving process?

- What have others done in similar situations?

- What should be done?

- How should it be done?

- Where should it be done?

- When should it be done?

- Who should do it?

- What milestones can best mark your progress?

- How will you know when you are successful?

Nearly all these questions can be helpful to consider when we deal with challenging situations in ministry. Our ability to find creative solutions to the problems we face often depends on asking the right questions.

SO-NOT-DONE QUESTIONS

1. What drives your students crazy and what makes them especially cheerful?

2. What would your youth ministry's epitaph be if it closed up shop tomorrow?

3. Imagine you've just received $10 million to help your ministry grow and prosper. How would you spend it?

4. What animal would you choose as your youth ministry emblem—and why?

5. Is there a way you can reword a problem or opportunity you are working on?

CREATIVE YOUTH LEADERS SEARCH FOR MORE THAN ONE ANSWER.

We've just finished looking at the importance of asking lots of questions and paying attention to how we phrase those questions. But it's also important to realize most good questions have more than one worthwhile answer. When we assume we've already got the "right" answer to a particular question, we limit possibilities and inhibit creativity.

Think about how many photos a professional wedding photographer usually takes. Within the last year, both of my sons got married. As "father of the groom" I posed for dozens of photos—and the wedding photographers took hundreds of shots at each wedding and reception. More photos offer more possibilities. Ask questions that offer more possibilities in the answers. Quantity breeds quality. The more answers you come up with, the more likely you are to arrive at the best solution.

Here's an interesting experiment conducted by British psychologist Peter Watson that demonstrates how we tend to stop thinking when we believe we've found a problem's solution. Watson would present subjects with the following three numbers in sequence.

> "The best way to get a good idea is to have lots of ideas."
>
> LINUS PAULING, NOBEL LAUREATE IN BOTH CHEMISTRY AND PEACE.

2   4   6

He would ask subjects to determine the numeric rule for this sequence and to give other examples of numbers that follow the same rule. The subjects were told they could ask as many questions as they wished without penalty.

Watson found that, almost invariably, most people would initially say, "4, 6, 8," or some similar sequence. And Watson would say, "Yes, that is an example of the same number rule." Then they would say, "20, 22, 24" or "50, 52, 54" and so on—all numbers increasing by two. After getting affirmative answers to a few attempts, most subjects felt confident—without exploring alternative possibilities—that the rule was that the numbers increase by two.

In *A Whack on the Side of the Head*, Roger von Oech invites readers to look at the five figures below and select the one that is different from all the others.

How did you do? If you chose figure B, congratulations! You've picked the right answer. Figure B is the one that has all straight lines. Give yourself a pat on the back! Some of you, however, may have chosen figure C, thinking C is unique because it's the only one that's asymmetrical. And you are also right! C is the right answer. A case can also be made for figure A: It's the only one with no points. Therefore, A is the right answer. What about D? It is the only one that has both a straight line and a curved line. So, D is the right answer, too. And E? Among other things, E is the only one that looks like a projection of a non-Euclidean triangle into Euclidean space. It is also the right answer. In other words, each answer is correct—depending on your point of view.

Actually, the rule Watson was applying was much simpler. His rule was simply that the numbers would increase. So they could be 1, 2, 3, or 10, 20, 40 or 400, 678, 944. And testing such alternatives would be easy—all the subjects would have had to do was to say "1, 2, 3" and see whether the result was affirmed. Or try "5, 4, 3" and see if the answer was positive or negative. This would have told them a lot about whether their guess about the rule was accurate.

Watson made a profound discovery: People will process the same information over and over in the same way without searching for alternatives until proven wrong—even when there is no penalty for asking questions that elicit a negative answer. In his hundreds of repetitions of this experiment, Watson never had an instance in which someone suggested an alternative hypothesis to find out if it were true. In short, his subjects didn't even try to find out if there were a simpler rule—or *any* rule—other than the one they assumed was true.

Creative youth leaders don't think this way. The creative person is always seeking alternative ways to think about a subject. Even when the old assumptions are well established, the creative individuals and groups will invent new ways of thinking. If something doesn't work, they look at it several different ways until they find a new line of thought. It is this willingness to entertain different perspectives and alternative ideas that opens them up to new possibilities the rest of us don't see.

Unfortunately, most formal education trains us to look for one answer, the "right" answer. As I mentioned earlier, the school classroom is often just an elaborate game of "guess what the teacher is thinking." Instead of asking, "What is the answer?" to any question we face, we should ask, "What are the answers?" and "What are the possibilities?"

Once we think we know what works or can be done, it becomes hard for us to consider alternative ideas. Consider the high jump event in track and field. People had jumped over the high bar the same way since the sport began. Then one day Dick Fosbury came along and moved the whole sport forward by going over the bar backward. By taking a new approach, and realizing that the traditional answer wasn't the only possible answer, Fosbury revolutionized his sport.

> "By the time the average person finishes college, he or she will have taken over 2,600 tests, quizzes, and exams. The 'right answer' approach becomes deeply ingrained in our thinking. This may be fine for some mathematical problems where there is in fact only one right answer. The difficulty is that most of life isn't this way. Life is ambiguous; there are many right answers—all depending what you are looking for. But if you think there is only one right answer, then you'll stop looking as soon as you find one."
>
> ROGER VON OECH, *A WHACK ON THE SIDE OF THE HEAD*

> "Granny is sitting knitting. Susan who is three years old is upsetting Granny by playing around with the ball of wool. One parent suggests that Susan ought to be put into the playpen to keep her from annoying Granny. The other parent suggests that it might be a better idea to put Granny into the playpen to protect her from Susan."
>
> EDWARD DE BONO, *SERIOUS CREATIVITY*

SO-NOT-DONE QUESTIONS

1. Take a blank piece of paper and list at least 20 uses for duct tape. (If that sounds tough, remember that George Washington Carver discovered more than 300 different uses for the peanut). You can do this.

TEN QUALITIES OF CREATIVE YOUTH LEADERS

2. Brainstorm as many answers as you can to this classic question: How do you keep a fish from smelling? (Here are some possible answers to get you started)

   • Cook it as soon as you catch it

   • Wrap it in paper

   • Put it in the freezer

   • Burn incense

   • Leave it in cold water

   • Cut off its nose

3. Take each of the following phrases and finish the line:

   For example "Instead of having a water balloon fight at camp...have a Ziploc baggie water fight." (They are easier to fill.) Now it's your turn:

   Instead of teaching in a classroom...

   Instead of one person reading through the text...

   Instead of asking, "What did you get out of this?"...

   Instead of closing the meeting in prayer...

5 CREATIVE YOUTH LEADERS KNOW THE TIMES AND PLACES THAT FOSTER THEIR CREATIVITY.

Where and when are *you* most creative? The answer is different for each of us—but the most creative people usually know what times and places nurture their own creative energies.

If you're like me, you may find that your office is one of the least creative places. Take a little time and think about where you feel creative, and seek out that place when you need to be creative—and even when you don't. Those relaxed times when we aren't feeling so pressured are often the times when we're able to pull the best ideas out of the recessed corners of our minds.

Scott Adams, creator of the comic strip *Dilbert*, says he does his best creative work between 6 a.m. and 7 a.m. About one in ten people are early morning people like this. This doesn't mean they particularly like getting up in the morning, but they find their minds most alert at this time of the day.

About two in ten people are the complete opposite. They are most alert and productive in the evenings and on into the night hours. These night owls have no problem staying up past midnight—and often find they get their most productive ideas at an hour when others are fast asleep.

The rest of the population, 7 out of every 10 of us, find ourselves somewhere in between. Some find their creative sparks flying in the mid-morning; others in the afternoon, and others are early evening people. Sometimes these times of day change as we age.

The secret is to do most of your creative thinking at the time that suits you best. Make good use of your most creative hours, and leave the other times of the day for tasks that require less creativity.

SO-NOT-DONE QUESTIONS

1. What favorite places have you found to stimulate your creative juices flowing?

2. What are the best times of the day for you to unleash your creativity?

It's said that the human brain will hold certain kinds of information for less than 30 seconds. If something doesn't happen during that time, the information becomes lost. Who knows how many great ideas were never implemented because they never made it past that first 30 seconds?

One way to offset the limits of our short-term memory is by re-exposing ourselves to information we want to retain. For example, talking about an event immediately after it happens can be one of the best ways to remember it. It also helps to write ideas down as they come to you. You may also want to revisit ideas every so often, not only for memory but also for coming up with improvements.

Creative people start working on an idea and allow their minds to return to that idea throughout the next several days, weeks, months, and even years. Who hasn't completed a project, an assignment, or anything requiring some level of creativity, only to get a better idea once we were done?

We are generally too satisfied with continuing to do things the way they have been done. The Western notion of improvement has always been concerned with removing defects, overcoming problems, and putting faults right. The Japanese share this concern with removing obstacles, but this is only the beginning. As Joel Barker explains in his book, *Future Edge*, the Japanese concept of *kaizen* involves an ongoing search for continuous improvement. Japanese workers are encouraged to look at something that seems perfect and try to find ways to improve on it. The Toyota Motor Company gets something like 300 suggestions from each of its Japanese employees every year because they are continually trying to improve something that is already working well.

When I'm preparing Bible studies, I usually spend about a month working on four different weekly messages. Rather than finishing one message before I begin working on the next, I'm continually coming back to each message, adding new ideas by using various tricks shared in this book. Each of the messages is in a different stage of development. I use a similar process in writing books, only it stretches out over a longer period of time. Right now, as I'm working on this book, I'm also working on three other books. The four stages I go through in writing a message or a book are:

- Research: Deciding the topic and researching commentaries, other books, magazines, and the Internet
- Sorting: Organizing the material in a logical manner
- Initial Writing: Getting my ideas on paper
- Editing and Delivery: Shaping the ideas and presenting them

Multitasking is one of the great buzz words today, but developmental molecular biologist John Medina says it's a bit of a myth—the brain really can focus on only one thing at a time. Sure, you can walk and chew gum at the same time, but when it comes to things that really require the brain's primary attention, the brain processes information sequentially. We can jump back and forth from one thing to another, but there is a small amount of time between thoughts—it's not all happening at the same moment in time.

One illustration of how we think sequentially is found when people drive while talking on a cell phone. Studies have shown that drivers who are talking on cell phones miss more than 50 percent of the visual cues spotted by attentive drivers. This alone is a great argument for never talking or texting on your cell phone while driving—and it may have been the reason California Governor Arnold Schwarzenegger signed legislation in 2008 prohibiting the use of handheld mobile phones while driving in the state (unless a hands-free device is used).

Multitasking may seem efficient but it is often counterproductive. According to Jeff White, it weakens short-term memory and makes you think slower. Some studies show it can actually kill brain cells. It is also a first-degree creativity killer. That's because creativity needs focus. You need to give your mind a chance to think clearly and openly—without distractions.

I think a better term than multitasking would be "task switching." People with good memories can pay attention to several inputs one at a time, regularly switching their primary focus. Young people are more adapt at task switching than older adults. The contemporary world is full of nonstop action—instant messaging, text messaging, Facebook, Twittering, YouTube, cell phones, video games, animated billboards—yet most young people don't seem overwhelmed by it all. In fact, all the time spent on action video games may be one reason teens tend to be better at task switching. Players process information more quickly, are able to spot more images with brief visual stimulus, track more objects at once, and have better task switching abilities.

SO-NOT-DONE QUESTIONS

1. What system do you use—or could you use—to help make sure your best ideas get revisited rather than forgotten?

2. How are you at task switching?

3. Are you able to focus on several issues over a period of time, continuing to return to each issue?

4. What projects are you working on now?

CREATIVE YOUTH LEADERS AREN'T AFRAID TO FAIL.

Someone once said, "You can fail many times, but you're not a failure unless you quit trying." One of Sir Winston Churchill's shortest and most famous speeches carried a similar message eloquently delivered in just three words: "Never give up." Creative people are like postage stamps—they stick to something until it gets where it needs to go.

Perseverance, however, doesn't mean continually pursuing dead-end paths, beating dead horses, or repeating things that haven't worked. Perseverance means working smart with the notion that you will keep taking the "one more time" approach until you cross the finish line.

Earlier in the book, I mentioned Dr. Seuss. Did you know that more than 20 publishers rejected his first children's book? Had Dr. Seuss quit instead of continuing to contact other publishers, his phenomenal success might never have occurred. His efforts with all those other publishers could easily be considered a series of failures, but by persevering he became a widely known author who's sold millions of books.

Remember Reggie Jackson, the baseball player? That guy could hit home runs. He knocked 563 balls into the seats during his 21-year major league career. Right now, that's good for eleventh place on the all-time list for career home runs. But Jackson is number one on another all-time list. He struck out more than any other player in baseball history—2,597 times in all.

Swinging involves taking risks and accepting that you'll sometimes fail. Ideas are like home runs. You've gotta take a swing at a bunch of ideas if you're ever gonna knock one out of the park.

The June 28, 1993, issue of *Newsweek* reported the findings of a study by Dean Keith Simonton of the University of California, Davis. Simonton looked at more than 2,000 of the greatest scientists throughout history and found that the most respected thinkers not only produced more great works—they also produced more "bad" ones. The greatest scientists of history "just kept working at it," Simonton concluded. "They produced."

TEN QUALITIES OF CREATIVE YOUTH LEADERS

The most creative people in the fields of art and science work obsessively. You've probably heard the story that Isaac Newton discovered gravity by sitting under an apple tree and waiting for the fruit to fall, but he didn't just spend his days lazing around under trees. His theories were the products of hard work and painstaking effort. "When inspiration does not come to me," Sigmund Freud once said, "I go halfway to meet it." Consider the efforts of these other creative thinkers:

- Bach wrote a cantata every week, even when he was sick or exhausted.

- Mozart produced more than 600 pieces of music.

- Einstein is best known for his paper on relativity, but he published 248 other papers.

- Darwin is known for his theory of evolution, but he wrote 119 other publications in his lifetime.

- Freud published 330 papers.

- Pablo Picasso produced between 20,000 and 50,000 pieces of art.

- Richard Branson has started 250 companies, not all of them successful.

- Rembrandt produced around 650 paintings and 2,000 drawings.

William Shakespeare wrote 154 sonnets. Some were masterpieces, others were no better than his contemporaries, and others were panned by critics. In fact, it's probably safe to say that more bad poems are composed by the major poets than by the minor poets. Major poets composed more bad poems simply because they produced more poetry.

Thomas Edison once said, "Genius is 1 percent inspiration and 99 percent perspiration." His own work is proof of the creative power of hard work and persistent effort. Edison filed a record 1,093 patents. His New Jersey laboratory contains a staggering display of hundreds of phonograph horns of every shape, size, and material. This collection of rejected ideas is a visual testament to Edison's thinking strategy to explore every imaginable possibility. For every brilliant idea that came together, Edison had many flops.

Edison conducted more than 9,000 experiments to develop the light bulb and more than 50,000 experiments to develop the storage fuel cell battery. Once, when an assistant asked why he continued trying to discover a long-lasting filament for the light bulb after thousands of failures, Edison responded by saying he didn't understand the question. In his mind, he hadn't failed even once; instead, he'd discovered thousands of things that didn't work.

Edison once declared, "Many of life's failures are people who did not realize how close they were to success when they gave up." Self-made billionaire Ross Perot expressed a similar thought when he said, "Most people give up when they're about to achieve success; they give up at the last minute of the game, one foot from the winning touchdown."

Few people deserve the title "creative genius" more than Albert Einstein. His theory of relativity is one of the greatest intellectual achievements in human history. Academically, however, Einstein was less than mediocre. One teacher told him he would "never amount to anything." Eventually, he was asked to leave school. After spending some time traveling in Italy, Einstein applied to the Zurich Polytechnic School but failed the admissions exam and was required to return to high school for a year before being accepted. After graduating from Zurich, he was rejected for an assistantship because no professor would give him a recommendation. He managed to get a job as a tutor but was soon fired.

He eventually got a job in the patent office. In his spare time, he continued his studies, quietly earned a doctorate, and began publishing his scientific findings. Finally, after many years in relative obscurity, his work won him the recognition he deserved. If Einstein had accepted his teachers' assessment of his intelligence, the world would be unimaginably poorer.

Consider these additional examples featured in the "Famous Failures" video at bluefishtv.com:

- Lucille Ball was dismissed from drama school with a note that said she was "wasting her time" and was "too shy to put her best foot forward."

- The Beatles were turned down by an executive from Decca Records who said he didn't like their sound and that guitar music was "on the way out."

- Ulysses S. Grant was a failed soldier, farmer, and real estate agent who, at age 38, went to work for his father.

- Michael Jordan was once cut from the high school basketball team. He went home, locked himself in his room, and cried.

- Walt Disney was fired from his job at a newspaper by people who said he lacked imagination and had no original ideas.

- Abraham Lincoln endured the death of his fiancée, two failed businesses, a nervous breakdown, and defeats in eight elections.

Creative people are not afraid of ridicule or failure. They have the courage of their convictions and are willing to wait for long periods before being rewarded for their accomplishments. Many great artists have found their creativity rejected, ignored, or even belittled. Vincent Van Gogh sold one painting in his lifetime—to his brother Theo. Consider how many scientists, artists, and writers were ridiculed or overlooked, only to be recognized for their significant contributions many years later.

Dick Liebhaber, executive vice president of MCI, once observed: "We do not shoot people who make mistakes. We shoot people who do not take risks." Innovativeness requires a certain tolerance for risk.

> "Comparing the lives and works of well-known individuals reveals a number of interesting findings. For instance, what did Hans Christian Anderson, Alexander Graham Bell, George Burns, Winston Churchill, Leonardo da Vinci, Walt Disney, Thomas Edison, Albert Einstein, Henry Ford, General George S. Patton, and Jack Welch have in common? All were dyslexic. Dyslexia is a condition in which written letters and numbers are perceived backwards. This can result in patterns that are confusing. Michelangelo experienced symptoms of bipolar disorder and depression. In spite of these disabilities all of these individuals found ways to learn and became outstanding achievers."
>
> ALAN J. ROWE, *CREATIVE INTELLIGENCE*

SO-NOT-DONE QUESTIONS

1. How willing are you to step out and take chance in your ministry?

2. Have you ever gone back and retried something that was unsuccessful the first time? What happened? What did you learn from your first failed attempt?

3. How do you feel about Thomas Edison's statement, "Genius is 1 percent inspiration and 99 percent perspiration"?

AWAKENING YOUR CREATIVITY

8 CREATIVE YOUTH LEADERS LOVE TO LAUGH AND HAVE FUN.

"More than four decades of study by various researchers confirms some common-sense wisdom: Humor, used skillfully, greases the management wheels," writes Fabio Sala in the *Harvard Business Review.* "It reduces hostility, deflects criticism, relieves tension, improves morale, and helps communicate difficult messages." According to the research, the most effective executives employed humor twice as often as middle-of-the-pack managers.

I think the same principle is equally true—or maybe even *more* true— when it comes to people in youth ministry. The most effective youth workers, the ones with the most creative ideas and programs, tend to be people who employ humor.

Southwest Airlines is one of today's most successful carriers, earning regular profits while many of its competitors wobble on the edge of insolvency. Southwest's former CEO Herb Kelleher once described what the company is seeking when hiring new employees: "What we are looking for, first and foremost, is a sense of humor. We don't care that much about education and expertise, because we can train people to do whatever they have to do. We hire attitudes." Southwest Airlines' mission statement? "People rarely succeed at anything unless they are having fun doing it."

On a recent Southwest flight from Sacramento to Orange County, I witnessed a wonderful expression of creativity. The lead flight attendant had asked the four children who boarded early if they would be willing to distribute small bags of peanuts during the flight. They were excited at the possibility, but he told them he could pick only one child. He devised a contest in which he took four sealed decks of cards and wrote the name of one of the kids on each deck. He announced to all the passengers just before takeoff that he was going to place the four decks of cards on the floor at the front of the plane. The child whose name was on the deck that slid to the back of the plane first would get to distribute the peanuts.

The game was so much fun. Everyone on the plane got into it—watching those four packs of cards slide down the aisle, slowly at first as the plane went down the runway, and then more and more quickly as the plane gained

speed and lifted off. The passengers were cheering and laughing. When the decks arrived at the back of the plane, the flight attendant announced that all four kids were winners, and they'd all help distribute the peanuts.

During his time as Southwest's CEO, Herb Kelleher was known for impersonating Elvis Presley and Roy Orbison at company parties. On one Halloween he came to Southwest's hangar in a dress, impersonating Corporal Klinger (from the television show *M*A*S*H*), to thank mechanics for working overtime. British Airways has hired its own "corporate jester" to help instill the airline with a greater sense of fun.

Jerry Greenfield, cofounder of Ben & Jerry's Ice Cream, has said, "If it isn't fun, why do it?" Joanne Carthey, who founded the software company NetPro (now owned by Quest), once announced that the company has four rules: "We make promises, we keep our word, we clean up our messes, and we have fun."

I am convinced that getting into a spirit of humor and fun not only loosens you, it enhances your creativity. For example, consider this riddle: What do John the Baptist and Winnie the Pooh have in common? Answer: They both have the same middle name. You'll never solve that little riddle if you're not in a playful frame of mind. And that spirit of fun and laughter is essential as we seek creative solutions to the bigger challenges we face.

Mike Yaconelli, the cofounder of Youth Specialties, was one of the most creative youth pastors I've ever met. He was also the epitome of this spirit of playfulness and fun I'm talking about. Mike knew the value of humor—it was part of the center of his being. I remember going with him to a restaurant in Joplin, Missouri, after we'd done a seminar together. There was a crowd at the entrance, with lots of people entering and leaving. I watched Mike grab a potted plant from a counter and hand it to a middle-aged couple as they went out the door. "Congratulations," Mike said, "you are our 5,000th customer." The couple was delighted. As they walked out the door with the plant, the group of us with Mike just broke into laughter.

I've watched Mike pay the highway toll for the car driving behind ours, even though he did not know the people following us. Then he'd watch in the rearview mirror as the toll collector explained to the people in the next car that their "friend" in the car ahead of them had already paid their toll.

In another restaurant I watched him put the table silverware up one of his sleeves and then let the silverware fall out of his sleeve onto the floor when a waiter walked by. With a look of profound embarrassment on his face, he'd start apologizing profusely, as if he'd just been caught trying to steal the silverware.

I have heard that Mike used to keep one of those remote-controlled devices that make a loud farting noise in his office. When a new employee was about to be hired, the final step was to meet Mike. He would put the gadget under the chair in front of his desk before inviting the prospective employee in. As Mike sat behind his desk asking questions, every so often he'd press the button that would trigger the little unit under the person's chair to sound off. He was too funny. He made Youth Specialties a fun place to be.

Mike's playfulness encouraged the creativity of those around him and freed them to think in new ways. People close to Mike felt comfortable to express unique ideas. Mike and his cofounder Wayne Rice started an annual convention for youth workers that was always held in a fancy hotel. He felt youth workers who often worked for little money deserved to have a convention in a nice place. He and Wayne also started one-day training events that traveled around the country. Some of the most creative ideas for youth ministry came from these events. I think Mike's playfulness was a big part of what freed up his mind to find innovative approaches to youth ministry.

SO-NOT-DONE QUESTIONS

1. When was the last time you laughed out loud?
2. Are you able to laugh at yourself?
3. Who do you admire who has a good sense of humor?

TEN QUALITIES OF CREATIVE YOUTH LEADERS

We sometimes get the idea that creative people always work from scratch. The painter stands in front of a blank canvas with paints, brushes, and pure inspiration and proceeds to create a picture that's nothing like anything that's ever been seen before, right? The artist simply closes her eyes, imagines something that's never existed in any form, and then makes it a reality. Isn't that how it always happens?

Maybe that describes how some painters work. But a lot of artists—probably most artists—use things that already exist as starting points for their own creative efforts. A painter might look at a bowl of fruit and seeks to portray every nuance of its lighting and shadows. Or maybe she stands in the middle of a field and paints the landscape right in front of her. Perhaps she tries to make her painting an exact copy of what she sees. Or maybe she goes for something more abstract, using brighter colors and radical shapes.

Some artists work from photographs. My niece, Bianca Martinez, is an artist who was asked to create an advertisement for an upcoming jazz festival. She found a photograph of one of the musicians scheduled to perform at the event and transformed that photo into a work of art.

AWAKENING YOUR CREATIVITY

Only God can create something out of nothing. I would suggest starting your creative process by tweaking something that already exists, by copying and adapting it to your surroundings and needs. Sometimes being creative simply means learning how to "copy right." Copy something already in existence and adapt it to your setting. Take something old and transform it into something new. Just about everything that seems "brand new" is really an addition or modification of something that already existed. Originality and creativity occurs when you adapt an existing idea to your specific problem or situation.

Collect and store ideas like a pack rat. Keep a container (a shoe box, desk drawer, or file folder) of ideas and idea starters. Begin collecting interesting announcements, quotes, designs, questions, images, cartoons, pictures, doodles, and words that might trigger your own thinking. Thomas Edison put it this way: "Make it a habit to keep on the lookout for novel and interesting ideas that others have used successfully." Thomas Edison used a screw cap in a new fashion when he and his team developed the fixture for the light bulb.

> "As 'made in God's image' creatures, we are all creative—no theological way around that. But I find that so many think creativity demands an *ex nihilo* magic, a new thing out of nothing (like God's creation of the world). Not so, fellow creative creatures! Most of the best creativity in youth ministry comes from modifying, tweaking, and customizing existing ideas to meet the specific needs of our students."
>
> MARK OESTREICHER, IN *THE CORE REALITIES OF YOUTH MINISTRY* BY MIKE YACONELLI

Creativity takes what we already know, adapts it, and puts it in a new setting—making something new from something old. In *The Core Realities of Youth Ministry*, Mike Yaconelli offers this example from when he first started in youth ministry,

> "The other leaders and I were trying to create a new way of doing evangelism. We wanted to find creative ways of attracting a crowd of teenagers to an event where we could present the gospel in a new way. What we came up with was a hayride (an old idea) but with a modern twist (adapted). In order to update this old idea and make it more attractive to teens, we decided to call it 'the world's largest hayride' and haul kids around with 18-wheeler trucks covered with hay. Instead of driving around in the hills, though, we decided to have the hayride downtown and drive through the city. We couldn't believe how many high

school students turned up—1,300! Something we hadn't counted on was the police coverage. They pointed out those 1,300 teenagers throwing hay over the road and at other cars was a problem, so we spent all night on the world's largest cleanup. Because of insurance issues and SUVs, this probably wouldn't be possible today, but this (now old) idea can be creatively adapted."

In his book *Tinkertoys*, Michael Michalko points out that many modern inventions are adaptations of something that can be observed in the natural world:

- Helicopters: Hummingbirds can also hover and fly backwards.
- Hypodermic needles: A scorpion uses the pointed tip of its tail to inject poison.
- Sonar: Bats emit sounds that bounce off objects in their way.
- Anesthesia: Many snakes use venom to paralyze and desensitize their prey before eating it.
- Snowshoes: The caribou's feet are designed to skim over snow.
- Tanks: The turtle is a virtually impregnable mobile unit.
- Airplanes: Planes brake with flaps just as birds brake with tail feathers.

Ludwig von Beethoven developed his musical talent by often duplicating the works of others. His first compositions were clearly based on practice, imitation, and learning from what had been done before. Another example is "The Star Spangled Banner" which, even though it was written from a U.S. fortress that was being attacked by the Royal Navy, was essentially the same tune as a popular drinking song in English pubs. Many church hymns have similar stories. Luther and his colleagues often took familiar melodies that were sung in pubs and bars and gave them new words. Current Christian popular music often follows a similar pattern, resembling popular secular music with a religious message.

Sometimes one creative innovation inspires another. For example, in 1845, when Sir John Franklin hauled one of the newfangled "tin cans" of veal to the Arctic, he had to have a hammer and chisel on hand to open it. The cans kept food fresh, but people were using everything from pick axes to revolvers to get them open. It wasn't until 1885 that the British Army and

---

[1] Johansson reports that there are many different sources for this story, with no definitive version. The main source for this recounting comes from www.allthingscherokee.com.

Navy responded to concerns by offering the first can opener. More recently, other creative individuals improved on that idea by creating a can with a weak seam that causes the can to open when the tab is pulled.

When I started in youth ministry many years ago, the "lock-in" was already a popular youth event in most churches. A lock-in is an activity in which students and their youth leaders stay in one building or facility all night, perhaps from 7 o'clock in the evening to 7 o'clock the next morning. Kids watch movies and play basketball and swim in a pool and hear a band or speaker—and usually have a lot of fun.

I was thinking about how we could make these events even more enjoyable and decided to try a new twist on the old idea. So I created the All Nighter. Instead of staying in a single place all night, the All Nighter involved going to different places. We started out at the YMCA, then went to a small amusement park (with miniature golf and batting cages), then to a bowling alley, then to an auditorium to hear a band and speaker, then to the beach to watch the sun rise over the hills. It was a huge hit. The first year we had 68 students sign up; by year four we had 500 senior high students involved, and I had to rent 10 busses. It was a total blast, and it attracted a lot of kids who would never set foot in a church. I didn't create something new out of thin air; I simply tweaked something that already existed. You can do this!

"Mick Pearce, an architect with an interest in ecology, accepted an intriguing challenge from Old Mutual, an insurance and real estate conglomerate: Build an attractive, functioning office building that uses no air conditioning. Oh, and do it in Harare, the capital of Zimbabwe.... He achieved it by basing his architectural designs on how termites cool their tower like mounds of mud and dirt. What's the connection?

Termites must keep the internal temperature in their mounds at a constant 87 degrees in order to grow an essential fungus. Not an easy job since temperatures on the African plains can range from over 100 degrees during the day to below 40 at night. Still, the insects manage it by ingeniously directing breezes at the base of the mound into chambers with cool, wet mud and then redirecting this cooled air to the peak. By constantly building new vents and closing old ones, they can regulate the temperature very precisely.

Pearce interests clearly extend beyond architecture. He also had a passion for understanding natural ecosystems, and suddenly those two fields intersected. Pearce teamed up with engineer Ove Arup to bring this combination of concepts to fruition. The office complex called Eastgate, opened in 1996 and is the largest commercial/retail complex in Zimbabwe. It maintains a steady temperature of 73 to 77 degrees and uses less than 10 percent of the energy consumed by other buildings its size."

FRANS JOHANNSSON, *THE MEDICI EFFECT*

In my book *Best-Ever Games for Youth Ministry*, I suggest a number of ways you might put a new spin on a classic game. Try creating something new by adding one of these twists to an old game:

- Add a strobe light (be sensitive to kids who have epilepsy)
- Add a fog machine
- Change the boundaries
- Change the object of the game
- Change the locomotion (the way people move while playing the game)
- Change the location
- Change the amount of time to play the game
- Change the time of day

SO-NOT-DONE QUESTIONS

1. Try taking the familiar words of Psalm 23 and paraphrasing them:
   - As a skater
   - As a tech geek
   - As a jock
   - As a farmer or rancher
   - As a drama queen

2. What are some activities you do now in your ministry that might be given a fresh spin?

3. Suppose you've planning a game that requires a ball, and you realize at the last minute that you forgot to bring the ball. What could you do?

AWAKENING YOUR CREATIVITY

In his 1872 poem "The Walrus and the Carpenter," Lewis Carroll wrote:

> "The time has come," the Walrus said,
>
> "To talk of many things:
>
> Of shoes—and ships—and sealing-wax—
>
> Of cabbages—and kings—"

I'm not suggesting that your next Bible study should confuse and distract kids with a wide-ranging conversation about cabbage, shoes, and kings on ships. But much like the walrus and his eclectic list of discussion topics, creative thinkers often produce something new by bringing together previously unrelated ideas, objects, and services. The process of combining ideas or elements or parts of ideas is called *synthesis*—and some people believe it to be the essence of creativity. In 1831, behavioral scientist Charles Spearman observed that creativity is "a consequence of the fusion of two or more previously unrelated ideas." And just like when people join their talents together in the body of Christ, the end product is often greater, more creative, and more effective than the individual parts.

Johann Gutenberg is a classic example of building something new by combining two previously unconnected ideas. Gutenberg created the first printing press by bringing together elements of the wine press and the coin punch. The purpose of the coin punch was to leave an image on a small area, such as a gold coin. The wine press was, and still is, used to apply force over a large area to squeeze the juice out of grapes. One day Gutenberg, perhaps after drinking a glass or two of wine, asked himself, "What if I took a bunch of these coin punches and put them under the force of the wine press so they left their image on paper?" The result was the beginning of the printing press

> "Creativity is a lot like looking at the world through a kaleidoscope. You look at the same set of elements everyone else sees, but then reassemble those floating bits and pieces into an enticing new possibility."
>
> ROSABETH MOSS KANTOR, PROFESSOR OF BUSINESS ADMINISTRATION, HARVARD BUSINESS SCHOOL

TEN QUALITIES OF CREATIVE YOUTH LEADERS

and movable type. His method of producing movable type endured almost unchanged for five centuries.

Then there's Pablo Picasso. One day, he found an old bicycle outside his house. After looking at it for a little while, he took off the seat and the handlebars. Then he pieced them back together in a different way to create the head of a bull.

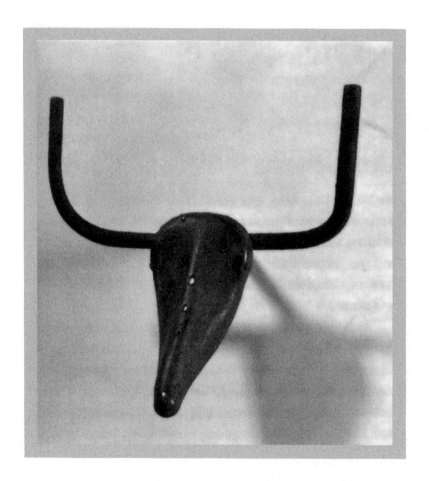

Leonardo da Vinci filled thousands of notebook pages with his ideas. These notebooks make it clear that one of da Vinci's techniques was to look for connections between two or more unrelated ideas. Once da Vinci was standing by a well and watched a stone hit the water at the same moment a bell chimed in a nearby church tower. He noticed the stone caused waves that

spread out in circles until they disappeared. By simultaneously concentrating on the circles in the water and the sound of the bell, he made the connection that led to his discovery that sound travels in "waves."

It is intriguing to speculate that the *Mona Lisa*, probably the most admired portrait in the world, may have been the result of da Vinci combining the best features of many beautiful faces that he'd observed. Perhaps this is why there has never been much agreement about the actual identity of the subject.

Da Vinci also suggested that you could find inspiration for marvelous ideas if you look into the stains on walls, ashes in a fire, the shape of clouds, and patterns in mud. He would imagine seeing trees, battles, landscapes, figures. According to his notebooks, da Vinci would even sometimes throw a paint-filled sponge against the wall and contemplate the stains.

When I think of this, I can't help but recall the scene from *Peanuts* where Charlie Brown, Lucy, and Linus are all lying on the ground looking up at the clouds. Lucy asks Linus what he sees, and he describes a series of elaborate and detailed scenes being played out in the clouds. Then she asks Charlie Brown the same question. He responds, "Well...I was going to say I saw a duckie and a horsie, but I changed my mind." There are times in my ministry when my own creative vision seems as limited as Charlie Brown's, and I have to remember not to give up.

> "Creativity is the ability to see relationships where none exist."
>
> THOMAS DISCH, AMERICAN SCIENCE FICTION AUTHOR AND POET

While working on his invention of the telegraph, Samuel Morris was stumped by the question of how to produce a signal strong enough to be received over great distances. Larger generators were insufficient because the signal would fade in proportion to the distance traveled. One day while riding a stage coach from New York to Baltimore, he saw tired horses being exchanged at a relay station. He made a connection and found the answer to his problem. The solution was to give the traveling signal periodic boosts of power. This insight made the coast-to-coast telegraph possible.

I've discovered a fun trick that combines a penny and a balloon. Place a penny inside a transparent latex balloon. Blow up the balloon and tie it off. Hold the balloon with one hand over the top near the knot or at the

"We were on an Ecuador mission trip a few years ago when one of my students reminded me how ingenious teenagers can be. Our task was to paint the roof of a Missionary Aviation Airport hanger. We took a compressed-air paint-spraying machine with us. Because we were so far back in the jungle and there was no way to get replacement parts, we kept praying that this machine would keep working. Sure enough, a couple of days into our work, the machine broke; a washer cracked and paint was seeping from the machine. Technology had failed us. What were we supposed to do now?

We searched for an extra washer with absolutely no luck. Then one of my students asked if he could have a button from the shirt of one of the men working with us. He cut the button off the man's shirt, walked to the drill press, and drilled a small hole in the middle of the button. We watched him as walked over to the paint machine and replaced the broken washer with the "button washer" he had just made. We had been lulled by technology into thinking that only mechanical parts would work. But we were wrong. That machine kept working without skipping a beat for the rest of the week, and we are able to complete our job thanks to the ingenuity and creativity of one student who was not limited by technology!"

DAVE AMBROSE, IN *THE CORE REALITIES OF YOUTH MINISTRY* BY MIKE YACONELLI

bottom of the balloon and begin to rotate your wrist. At first the penny will bounce around inside the balloon. If you keep going, eventually the penny will flip on its edge and begin rolling around the interior surface. Once the penny gets rolling, stop rotating your wrist and simply hold the balloon with your one hand over the top. The penny will zoom around for up to 3 minutes. Have your students try this and see how long they can keep the penny going. (You can also do this with a marble, but it won't keep moving as long.)

Then try putting other small objects in a balloon (such as small pieces of wrapped candy) and then tossing the off-balance balloon around the room. You'll be amazed at how much the slight weight will affect the balloon's flight. Charley Scandlyn and members of his youth group at Menlo Park Presbyterian Church created an ad for their upcoming ski trip by dubbing the voices of several students over the actual actors in a short clip from the movie *A Few Good Men*. It was very clever and funny.

SO-NOT-DONE QUESTIONS

Okay, now it's your turn to try combining objects to create something new. Choose any three items from the drawings on the next page and make up a sentence. For example, if you took an iron, snow, and a rose you might come up with "I took the iron and melted the snow on the mountain to water the rose." Got the idea? There are no wrong answers. Have fun.

AWAKENING YOUR CREATIVITY

84

Source: Marlene D. LeFever, *Creative Teaching Methods*

CATALYSTS
FOR CREATIVITY
CHAPTER FIVE

In scientific terms the word *catalyst* refers to a substance that speeds up a chemical reaction. Catalysts help get a process going and help it move along more smoothly or rapidly.

Often our creativity requires a catalyst—some kind of stimulus that can help get us moving and keeps our creative fires burning. In this chapter we'll take a look at some of the most important catalysts for creativity.

WHAT'S YOUR MOTIVATION?

It's simple: People who are strongly motivated to accomplish a task tend to be more creative than those who aren't. If you have a reason you want to get a job done—and to do it well—you'll approach that job with greater ingenuity and creativity.

But what kind of motivation really serves as the best catalyst for creativity? Motivation comes in two forms. The first, extrinsic motivation, refers to motivation that comes from the outside, and it has a long history of influencing behavior. B.F. Skinner did a number of well-known psychological experiments that illustrate the power of rewards as motivation. In the most famous of these, a rat is placed in a box containing a button and a food dispenser. If the rat steps on the button, it will get a reward—in this case, food pellets. The reward provides the motivation that drives the rat to keep stepping on the button to get more food.

Extrinsic motivation can include not just rewards but also negative forces, such as punishment. Guilt is one form of punishment that too many youth pastors use to try to motivate others. We threaten, frighten, snarl, growl, bristle, and become just

plain nasty in hopes of persuading students or adult volunteers to do what we hope they'll do.

So how effective are these external motivators in enhancing creativity? The answer: Not very effective. Even if the threat of punishment works to motivate people for a brief time, the problem is that once the pressure lets up, so does the response. And the same is true of rewards—once the reward is removed, so is the motivation.

Harvard Business School psychologist Teresa Ambile examined the effects of extrinsic rewards on creativity in a study involving more than 100 children. She found that the children who had no chance of getting a reward for solving a problem were able to do so significantly faster than the children who would receive a reward.

Intrinsic motivation tends to be far more effective in enhancing creativity. Intrinsically motivated people are self starters. They do not need the threat of punishment or the promise of reward to get them to be creative. Their motivation comes from within.

> "A group of extremely bright (average I.Q. of 158) young adults participated in a study to determine the effects of multiple types of sensory stimulation on creativity. Over a period of five weeks, experimental subjects were seated in a darkened room and stimulated with high-frequency signals from an oscillator, a rotating wheel, incense, a floor vibrator, and loud music. Each week, both before and after being stimulated, they were given five minutes to draw a picture of a vase of flowers, using pencil and crayons. A panel of artists judged the drawings made following stimulation to be more creative than those made before. Of course, it would be risky to generalize too much from this one study, particularly since the subjects were unusually intelligent (and young), but it does suggest that sensory stimulation may have beneficial effects on creativity."
>
> DOROTHY TAYLOR AND WALTER SAPP, *WHEN SPARKS FLY*

SENSING CREATIVITY

Being properly motivated is a key ingredient in the creative process, but it does not stand alone. I would encourage you to involve your senses in the creative process. Each of our five main senses—sight, hearing, taste, touch, and smell—can be used effectively used as a catalyst to enhance and expand our creativity.

First, let's look at (pun intended) the sense of sight. Seventy-five percent of the information humans receive about their environment comes from their sight, making it by far the most important of the five senses. Our sense of sight depends on the eyes to take in information and the brain to make sense

of what the eyes see. But sometimes the brain is deceived by information received from the eyes. The persuasive power of some images is so strong that it can lead us astray—they can even be used as instruments of propaganda. Here are some examples of visual images that can trick the brain:

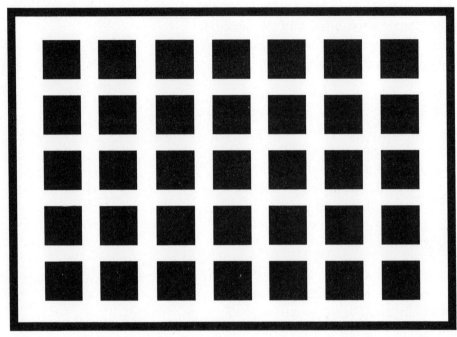

Do you see gray areas between the squares?

Are the horizontal lines parallel, or do they slope?

Count the black dots.

Although it's true that our eyes can sometimes trick us, visual images are also a primary way truth and information can be conveyed. Leonardo da Vinci used drawings, diagrams, and graphs as primary ways to capture information and to formulate and solve problems. In Leonardo's notebooks, the diagrams and drawings are the focal points, not the words. Language took a secondary role for Leonardo. He viewed language as a way to name or describe discoveries, but not as the primary path to make new discoveries.

Even though words evolved from pictures and symbols, that does not mean words are more advanced. As many people have said, a picture is worth a thousand words. Studies have shown that people remember pictures far better than they remember written or spoken words. So pump up those PowerPoint presentations with lots of graphics and images and cut back on the lengthy word slides.

Color is another very powerful visual communicator. God created color as one of nature's languages. Colors have meaning, and they speak volumes.

They affect our moods, stir emotions, and help us define our world. If we understand the fundamental meaning of colors, we can use them to enhance our experiences in both creativity and ministry.

The Dutch painter Vincent Van Gogh was very interested in how colors symbolized emotions. One example of his use of the power of color was through his famous paintings of his bedroom in Arles. Van Gogh painted the same scene three different times, varying only the colors.

Used with permission of the Museum d' Orsay, Paris, and the Van Gogh Museum, Amsterdam.

In a letter to his brother, Van Gogh describes in detail his color choices on one of these paintings:

> "This time it's just simply my bedroom, only here color is everything…. The walls are a pale violet. The floor is of red tiles. The wood of the bed and chairs is the yellow of fresh butter, the sheets and pillows very light greenish-citron. The coverlet scarlet. The window green. The toilet table orange. The basin blue. The doors lilac."

In other writings Van Gogh described what each color would represent. The white walls would evoke an atmosphere of quiet and dreaming. The red floor and ceiling would suggest warmth and inspiration. The yellow of the chair and bed were to be inviting and comfortable. The blue of the basin would suggest fresh water, while the green of the window frame recalls nature. Every color was chosen with awareness of its meaning, purpose, and emotional impact.

In his book *Holy Wow*, Jeff White suggests this basic color lexicon that can be used as a reference in your creative activities:

- Cyan (greenish-blue)   Cold, analytical, intelligent
- Sky Blue   Calm, true, honest
- Violent   Deep, thoughtful, reflective
- Purple   Royal, majestic, exciting
- Mauve   Stylish, cultured, impressive
- Pink   Sensitive, lovely, feminine
- Red   Powerful, aggressive, demands attention
- Orange   Stimulating, zesty, tangy
- Gold   Rich, sunny, joyful
- Yellow   Startling, anxious, sharp
- Lime   Youthful, fresh, naïve
- Green   Mature, strong, natural
- White   Pure, peaceful, sterile
- Black   Elegant, mysterious, serious

CATALYSTS FOR CREATIVITY

White suggests using specific colors as catalysts for creative work. For example, if you are focusing a session on a subject like relationships or sexual purity, you might print materials on red paper. If you're creating a lesson about choices, you might take advantage of neutral colors such as gray or light blue. Whether you are aware of it or not, color communicates—so make sure it's communicating what you intend.

Your productivity may be affected by the colors of your youth room, your office, and even your computer screen saver. In a 2008 study in *Science* magazine, researchers at the University of British Columbia tested groups of people looking at images or words displayed against red, blue, or neutral backgrounds on computer screens. The red group did better on tests of recall and attention for detail, such as remembering words or checking spelling or punctuation. The blue group did better on tests requiring invention and imagination, such as coming up with creative uses for a brick. Another study found that people attending a party were more likely to chose a yellow or red room over a blue room. Those guests in the red and yellow rooms were more social and active, yet guests who chose the blue room stayed longer.

Even though we may receive the majority of our information from our sense of sight, don't underestimate the effect of our other senses on creativity. Consider the sense of hearing. Studies have shown that different sounds and various kinds of music can actually slow down or speed up brain waves. Classical music and certain forms of jazz have shown a measurable ability to optimize cranial activity. But the amazing thing is that it doesn't matter what type of music you listen to—just about any music will help stimulate creative ideas.

The sense of touch is also tremendously important. Your skin contains a multitude of different receptors, including specialized nerve endings that sense things like pressure, vibration, tension, pain, and temperature. Your brain knows which kind of sensor is activated and where it is on the body because each sensor has a "private line" that carries only one kind of information to the brain. Some parts of your body are more sensitive than others. Your fingers contain more receptors than your elbows do, which is why you don't explore an object with your elbow when you are trying to figure out what it is.

Students (especially boys) like to be able to move around and touch and experiment with objects. So bring lots of physical objects into your youth group environment. And as long as we're talking about how things "feel," I would also add that we need to always consider how various experiences we plan will feel emotionally to our students.

Now let's involve the sense of taste. There are five basic flavors: Salty, sweet, sour, bitter, and umami. Umami is the savory taste that is found in cooked meat or mushrooms or in the food additive MSG (monosodium glutamate). There is not word for it in the English language, which is why we use the Japanese term. Taste can be a stimulating catalyst for creativity as well as a powerful way to experience Gods' truth. Psalm 34:8 says, "Taste and see that the Lord is good." The Bible is filled with references to taste, and many of them are figurative. God gave us the tongue with the most acute sensitivity of all our senses and uses many food metaphors in the Bible to help us understand his ways. Jesus seemed to like to use food as part of his teaching—consider the Last Supper with it's bread and wine, the miracles of the loaves and fishes, and many of his parables. Seems like he thought people would remember the lesson better if they tasted it.

Finally let's explore the sense of smell. Aromatherapy is popular for a reason—it works. Some scents are soothing and can calm the body and mind. More vivid odors can stimulate stronger responses.

"Remember your mother warning you not to listen to loud music because you'd ruin your ears? She was right. In the United States one-third of people over sixty and half of those over seventy-five have hearing loss. The most common cause is long term exposure to loud noises. Baby Boomers are losing their hearing earlier than their parents and grand parents did, presumably because our worlds are nosier then they used to be. Some experts are particularly worried about portable MP3 players like iPod, which can produce very loud music for hours without recharging."

SANDRA AAMONDT AND SAM WANG, *WELCOME TO YOUR BRAIN*

Smells can bring back a rush of highly intense memories. This is known as the Proust effect, named after Marcel Proust, a French author who wrote about how smells can recall long-lost experiences. Smells also have strong emotional associations—think about your grandmother's apple pie, the smell of burning leaves, or fresh coffee in the morning. Emotions incite action.

Good businesses understand the power of smell. It's been estimated that having the smell of chocolate in a candy store can raise chocolate sales by 60 percent. Starbucks does not allow employees to wear perfume on company time because it interferes with the seductive smell of the coffee they serve.

If a specific positive scent can spark a memory about a teenager's relationship with God, it'll leave an indelible—and even eternal—impression. But also be aware that smell can also have negative power. If the youth room smells unpleasant the first time a new student attends your group, there's a good chance that student won't want to return—and he may not even realize why!

Creative youth leaders recognize the importance of including multisensory experiences in youth group meetings. Multiple cues dished up via different senses speed up responses, increase accuracy, increase stimulation detection, and enrich encoding at the moment of learning.

Here's an exercise to get you thinking about how you might incorporate all the senses into your work with youth. Suppose you're planning a Christmas program. You might ask yourself or your team what comes to mind when you think of the word *Christmas*. You will probably get several responses. But I've found you can increase the number of responses by asking the following questions:

What does Christmas look like?
Examples: Trees, snow, light, angels, gifts

What does Christmas sound like?
Examples: Bells, laughter, carols, wrapping paper

What does Christmas taste like?
Examples: Chocolate, sweets, pumpkin pie, eggnog

What does Christmas smell like?
Examples: Cookies, pine, fudge, turkey, cider

AWAKENING YOUR CREATIVITY

What does Christmas feel like (physically)?
Examples: Cold outside, warm fireplace, snow

What does Christmas feel like (emotionally)?
Examples: Happy, festive, love, busy, sad, depressing, lonely

You can then take all these brainstormed ideas and create a talk or a skit, or decide on a theme to explore in your Christmas program. You'll come up with far more ideas this way then just asking for thought about "Christmas."

LET US PLAY

One of the most enjoyable ways to speed up creativity is through the use of play. Necessity may be the mother of invention, but play is certainly the father!

Play and exercise boost creativity because tiny proteins called BDNFs are created when you play and exercise. These proteins act like Miracle-Gro for your brain. Ample evidence points to the enormous health and professional benefits of laughter, lightheartedness, games, and humor. Of course, there is a time to be serious, too. But too much seriousness can be bad for your ministry and worse for your overall well-being.

"Play-Doh is an item that touches several sensory bases. Part of it is the smell, which sends me back to my childhood. Part of it is the way it feels-so submissive, squishy, and warm. Part of it is the way it looks-a big, bright, happy lump. It makes me want to do something with it. It gives me ideas."

DOUG HALL, *JUMP START YOUR BRAIN*

According to the *Wall Street Journal*, more than 50 European companies—including less-than-zany firms such as Nokia, Daimler-Chrysler, and Alcatel—have brought in consultants to help them use play to enhance creativity. These companies recognize that when we play, we become childlike and begin to behave in spontaneous, creative ways. Both play and creativity often involve using objects and actions in new or unusual ways.

One technique of some of these companies is to use Lego building blocks to train corporate executives. Lego was founded in 1932 by Ole Kurt Christiansen, who was a carpenter by trade. The name comes from fusing two Danish words: *leg* (meaning "play") and *godt* (meaning "well"). So *Lego*

means "play well." Ole made the first Lego blocks out of wood, and later switched to plastic after his original plant burned down. In 2008 the company celebrated its fiftieth anniversary of using the style of pieces we have today. It's estimated that the world's children spend 5 billion hours a year playing with these blocks—and I think most adults could benefit from spending a bit more time "playing well."

> "Never put off until tomorrow the fun you can have today."
>
> ALDOUS HUXLEY

C.S. Lewis once wrote, "When I was 10, I read fairy tales in secret and would have been ashamed if I had been found doing so. Now that I am 50, I read them openly. When I became a man, I put away childish things, including the fear of childishness and the desire to be very grown up." I think Lewis understood the truth of Proverbs 17:22: "A cheerful heart is good medicine, but a crushed spirit dries up the bones." You don't stop being playful because you get old—you get old because you stop being playful.

One of Walt Disney's greatest creative secrets was his ability to draw out the inner child in his business associates and combine it with their business expertise. Because he made the work fun, his associates worked and played together with a missionary zeal. Disney was a true genius who got the creative collaboration he needed by consciously creating a humorous and playful environment.

Einstein has been described as the perennial child. The great scientist was very much aware of the parallels between the thought patterns of creative thinkers and those of playful children. In fact, it was Einstein who suggested to Piaget that he investigate the way children think about speed and time, thereby inspiring one of the psychologist's most illuminating lines of research.

Here's a simple game created by one of my students, Josiah Gellsinger. He called the game WAG (Word Association Game). He would find students in his dorm or the cafeteria and have them sit in a circle or around a table. One student would start the game by saying aloud a word—any word. The person to the left of the first student would then say a word related in some way to the first person's. The next person would then say any word that came to mind in response to the word from the previous student, and so on. The words chosen often go in strange and unique directions. If a word doesn't seem closely associated with the previous word, any player can question it, and the person who said the word has to explain the association. I've seen students play this fun game for long periods of time. It helps them get to know one another better, stimulates the mind, and invites creativity.

IT'S ALL AROUND YOU

What does the physical environment that surrounds you have to do with creativity? It might say very little about creativity directly, but indirectly, it can communicate a lot. Your office and the youth group meeting room make powerful statements about the value the ministry places on creativity. The physical environment speaks to us loudly, if nonverbally.

You want your youth group meeting room and your office to be fun and wild and inviting and comfortable. Surround your rooms with stimulating, interesting objects to help create a fun, creative environment. Take a look at these youth rooms that were featured in a Youth Specialties CORE presentation (the motorcycle is being used as a podium):

At one time I had one of the world's largest collections of *Mad* magazines and other *Mad* collectables. My office used to be filled with these crazy items, but I've sold most of them in recent years. I've also had a couple of opportunities to visit the *Mad* offices on Madison Avenue in downtown Manhattan. What an interesting place! The minute you get off the elevator on their floor, you know this is a fun place. They are so many silly and intriguing things on the walls and on desks and hanging from office ceilings. Bill Gaines—publisher of *Mad* for more than 40 years—used to love Zeppelins and had an office full of them.

Bill also had a creative way of saving work time. At his desk he had an ink pad and a small metal stand with about 20 rubber stamps, each featuring a different phrase. Bill would often answer correspondence by stamping an incoming letter with one or more of these stamps, adding his signature, and then putting that same letter back in a new envelope and returning it to the sender.

Bill Gaines and Les Christie in 1985

The Youth Specialties offices have moved recently, but their old headquarters in El Cajon, California, used to exhibit a similar kind of creative craziness. There was fun stuff everywhere, with everyone's workspace or office looking just a little different. The break room had a 1950s theme, with a jukebox and brightly colored furniture. Environments like that call forth creativity.

You want both your youth group room and your office to be the kind of place that draws kids together. The best youth rooms resemble a watering hole in Africa—where animals who might have no other reason to gather will come together and hang out, including gazelles with giraffes and zebras with elephants. I've heard that if there's a severe drought, a wildebeest may even chance a drink when the lions are across the pond. Youth ministry watering holes include not only your offices and youth rooms but also any place that brings youth together on an informal, unpredictable basis.

SOMETHING NEW IN THE EVERYDAY

This may seem disarmingly obvious—but many times we miss the catalysts for creativity that are present in our everyday experiences. In 1887, John Boyd Dunlop noticed his son was finding it very uncomfortable to ride his tricycle over cobblestone streets. The stimulus of a garden hose (an everyday object) pulsing with water gave him an idea. He wrapped a hollow rubber tube around the rims of the two wheels on his bicycle and pumped them full of air and invented the pneumatic tire.

Growing up in West Los Angeles in the '50s gave me an opportunity to see some neat firsts. I had a chance to visit Disneyland with my family the first year it opened. One of the first rides I went on was the Jungle Cruise boat ride. I still remember the tour guide's comment as we went behind a waterfall: "Today, you get to see the backside of water." We were getting a different perspective on something we see every day.

The reality is that we miss an awful lot of what surrounds us in our daily experiences. But when we really pay attention, we often find something significant or different. A famous experiment demonstrated how people can fail to see what's right in front of them. In this experiment performed in 1999, Daniel Simons and Christopher Chabris asked people to watch a video clip and count the number of times two teams of basketball players passed the ball around. As they focused on the player passing the ball, almost half of the observers failed to notice a man in a gorilla suit who entered from the right

and exited the left. The clip demonstrated that we often fail to see what we don't pay attention to, even when it's in front of our eyes. We only perceive a fraction of what is going on in the world around us.

Here's another example of how we sometimes fail to see what's right in front of us. Read the following:

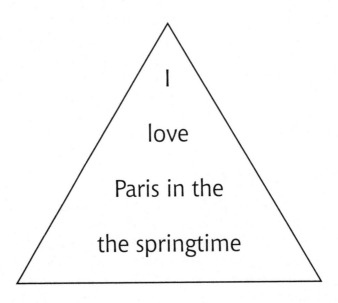

I

love

Paris in the

the springtime

Since the words *I love Paris in the springtime* are very familiar to most people, they often fail to notice that the word *the* appears twice. However, if you concentrate on reading one word at a time and see what's there (rather than what you are expecting to see), the second *the* is easy to notice.

Consider the FedEx logo that's printed on the sides of the delivery company's trucks. You have probably seen that logo thousands of times. Let me ask you three questions about it.

- What is the color of the "Fed" in the logo?
- What is the color of the "Ex"? (Did you get both questions? See, you're doing great!)
- Now, what is the color of the arrow?

Are you asking, "What arrow?" Next time you see one of these trucks, look closely at the white area between the *E* and the *x* in the sign. You will never see that FedEx logo the same way again.

Or check out a package of Hershey's Kisses. Did you ever notice the Hershey's kiss in the logo itself? If not, keep looking—you'll find it between the *k* and the *i*.

Make a conscious effort in your everyday, ordinary life to try to look at things differently. Whether you are walking, doing yard work, cleaning, cooking, bike riding, or driving, try to pause and look around whenever you can. You may find something you'd never noticed before.

Thomas Edison, while pondering how to make a carbon filament, was mindlessly toying with a piece of putty, turning and twisting it in his fingers. When he looked down at his hands, the answer hit him: Twist the carbon like a rope.

Rarely, if ever, does anyone create something completely new. Even Einstein's theory of relativity was not so much a new creation as it was a discovery of what was already there. But Einstein saw what others couldn't see; he saw the facts in a new way. He invented a new way of looking at how the world works.

When we look at our churches and youth programs in a new light or from a completely different angle, we may find new ways of ministering that will knock the socks off our kids and our congregations. One group I know started a boxing club and Bible study. This group understood the Bible study as part of the discipline required to be a fighter, and God continues to use this powerful ministry. Another youth worker I know developed a youth program that builds and races cars in the local racing circuit. What great ways to re-envision youth group activities!

Like an artist who steps pack from his painting to get a new perspective, find way to look at everyday items from different viewpoints. Sometimes stepping away from a task for a period of time can give you the new perspec-

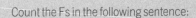
Count the Fs in the following sentence:

FINISHED FILES ARE THE RESULT OF YEARS OF
SCIENTIFIC STUDY COMBINED
WITH THE EXPERIENCE OF YEARS.

"If you found less than six, you probably ignored the Fs in the word *of*. If so, you are probably thinking, 'Of course, it was right before my eyes the whole time.' Ordinarily we do not make the fullest use of our ability to see. We look at a subject and do not see the details. And the details sometimes contain the germ of an idea that will lead to a creative breakthrough."

MICHAEL MICHALKO, *CRACKING CREATIVITY*

tive you need. Time away is crucial for the creative process. When you are struggling to come up with a solution or new direction, sometimes you may want to release the tension by stepping back from the immediate problem or opportunity.

Leonardo da Vinci believed it was essential to view something from a minimum of three different perspectives to have a basis for understanding it. For example, when he designed the first bicycle, he looked at this new form of transportation from the viewpoint of an inventor, then from the viewpoint of the investors who would sponsor prototypes and production, then from the viewpoint of the bicycle rider.

A simple reversal of angles dramatically changes what we see. When Henry Ford went into the automobile business, the conventional thinking was that you had to "bring people to the work." He reversed this to "bring the work to the people"—and invented the assembly line.

TO ERR IS CREATIVE!

History is full of examples of important new ideas that came about through chance, misfortune, error, or "foolishness." Next time something doesn't go as you'd hoped, pay attention—you may be on the verge of a creative breakthrough!

Many advances in medicine were the result of opportunistic observations. For example, the process of immunology was discovered by Louis Pasteur when an assistant made a mistake and gave too weak a dose of cholera bacteria to some chickens. This weak dose seemed to protect the chickens against the fuller dose that was given later.

Most school kids can tell you that when explorer Christopher Columbus first reached the shores of North America, he mistakenly believed he'd made it all the way around the world and landed in the Indies. But did you know that Columbus attempted that voyage westward to the Indies only because he was using the wrong measurement? He was using the calculations derived from Ptolemy's erroneous measurement of the circumference of the globe. Had he known the correct measurements, which had been worked out by Erathostenes (who lived in Alexandria before Ptolemy), Columbus would probably never have set sail, because he'd have known his ships could not have carried sufficient provisions.

Teflon was an accidental discovery made by Roy Plunkett while working for DuPont in 1938. Hoping to invent a new refrigerant, Plunkett instead created a glob of white waxy powder that conducted heat and failed to stick to surfaces. He abandoned his original line of research and continued experimenting with this fascinating material, which eventually became the hugely winning Teflon. Things like this happen when you give yourself the freedom to see what you weren't looking for.

Alexander Fleming wasn't the first physician to notice the mold that formed on an exposed culture when he was studying deadly bacteria. Less gifted physicians routinely ignored this seemingly irrelevant event, but Fleming noted it as "interesting" and wondered if it had potential. This interesting observation led to the development of the first antibiotic, penicillin, which has saved millions of lives.

> "In 1904, Antoine Feutchwanger was selling sausages at the Louisiana Exposition. First he tried offering them on individual plates, but this proved too expensive. He then offered his customers white cotton gloves to keep the franks from burning their fingers. The gloves were expensive, too, and customers tended to walk off with them. Antoine and his brother-in-law, a baker, sat down to figure out what inexpensive item could be added to the frankfurter to prevent people from burning their fingers. His brother-in-law said something like, 'What if I baked a long bun and slit it to hold the frank? Then you can sell the franks, and I can sell you the buns. Who knows, it might catch on.'"
>
> MICHAEL MICHALKO, *TINKERTOYS*

Michelangelo's masterpiece, David, was partially the result of another sculptor's failed attempt. Back in 1463, authorities at the Cathedral of Florence acquired a 16-foot-high chunk of white marble to be carved into a sculpture. Two well-known sculptors worked on the piece and gave up, and the badly mangled block was put in storage. Forty years later Michelangelo took the "ruined" marble out of storage, and within 18 months he carved it into one of the world's greatest statues.

So when things don't turn out as you'd planned, keep your senses open because those anomalies may trigger new ideas and new insights. Chance discoveries favor the open, active mind that is consciously searching for connections. George de Mestral, the Swiss inventor, was not the first person to notice how cockleburs stick to clothes. But his curiosity was provoked, and when he examined the burr with his microscope, he saw that it had hundreds of tiny hooks that snagged the loops of thread of his socks. Armed with that knowledge, he invented Velcro.

CATALYSTS FOR CREATIVITY

Whenever you're feeling stale and bored, try a change of scenery to inspire you. Go to a nature store, a dollar store, Brookstone store, Sharper Image store, trade show, library, museum, flea market, nursing home, toy store, or high school. Pick up something at random and create connections and relationships in your mind with the object and your problem. Wander around with an open mind and wait for something to catch your attention. It will.

Many successful people report that their best ideas come when they are not thinking about solving problems. Prepare to be surprised. Expect the unexpected. The key at times in life is to acknowledge the occasional disappointments and challenges life presents and face them head on.

IT'S KIND OF LIKE…

Another creative catalyst that can help inspire new ways of thinking is comparison. By taking something which is unfamiliar and comparing it with something more familiar, we can increase our understanding and shed new light on unknown situations.

The Bible is full of comparisons—analogies, similes, and metaphors—all intended to inspire new ways of thinking. Jesus began many of his parables with the phrase "The Kingdom of God is like…" and then he would use familiar words and images to help his listeners understand what can't be fully understood. And throughout the Scriptures God is described using comparisons. Jesus did this constantly, comparing God to a woman who had lost a coin or a father eagerly awaiting the return of his son—and in doing so, he gave his listeners a new vision of what God is like.

We see lots of comparisons in the book of Proverbs, especially chapters 25-27. In *A Whack on the Side of the Head*, Roger von Oech offers the following quiz using verses from Proverbs. See if you can connect these metaphors from Proverbs with the ideas they represent—and if you're not sure, look up the verses!

METAPHOR	IDEA
1. A constant dripping on a rainy day (27:15)	A. Kind words
2. A cool day in the hot summertime (25:13)	B. A fool that repeats his folly
3. Chewing with a sore tooth (25:19)	C. A faithful employee
4. A cloud blowing over the desert without dropping any rain (25:14)	D. Interfering in an argument that isn't your business
5. A city with broken-down walls (25:28)	E. A stimulating friendly discussion
6. Yanking a dog's ears (26:17)	F. A good man who compromises with a wicked one
7. Sparks that fly when iron strikes iron (27:17)	G. A man without self-control
8. Honey (16:24)	H. A cranky woman
9. Polluting a stream (26:25)	I. A person who doesn't give the gift he promised
10. A dog that returns to his vomit (26:11)	J. Confiding in an unreliable person

Often we can use a familiar word or phrase to provide a visual image that helps explain something unfamiliar. For example, when the engineers at Dolby Labs first developed noise-reduction technology back in the late 1960s, they needed an image to help people understand what the process could do. So they compared the process to a washing machine, which washed the dirt (noise) out of the clothes (signal); in the same way, noise reduction got rid of the hiss and other unwanted noise and cleaned up the sound. That metaphor gave us a new point of view by using something known to explain something unknown.

Steve Jobs once explained the benefits of a personal computer by comparing the computer to a bicycle. The bicycle amplifies our ability to get from one place to another. The computer amplifies our intelligence.

Sometimes a comparison can provide a visual image to explain an idea. Captain Grace Hopper was a computer pioneer who taught at Harvard, Bernard, and Vassar, and worked on Univac (one of the first computers ever developed). She was once asked to explain a nanosecond. A nanosecond is a

CATALYSTS FOR CREATIVITY

billionth of a second, and it's the basic time interval of a computer's internal clock. She explained it by using a piece of string that was 11.8 inches long. That string represented the distance light travels in one billionth of a second. It gave people a way of visualizing a billionth of a second. (Hopper is also famous for coining an expression familiar to many of us in ministry: "It is easier to ask forgiveness than it is to get permission.")

A fifth-grade teacher in a Christian school asked her class to look at TV commercials and see if they could use them in some way to communicate ideas about God. Here are some of the results:

- God is like...Bayer Aspirin. He works miracles.
- God is like...Ford. He's got a better idea.
- God is like...Coke. He's the real thing.
- God is like...Hallmark cards. He cares enough to send his very best.
- God is like...Tide. He gets the stains out that others leave behind.
- God is like...General Electric. He brings good things to life.
- God is like...Sears. He has everything.
- God is like...Alka-seltzer. Try him, you'll like him.
- God is like...Scotch tape. You can't see him, but you know he's there.
- God is like...Delta. He's ready when you are.
- God is like...Allstate. You're in good hands with him.
- God is like...VO-5 hair spray. He holds through all kinds of weather.
- God is like...Dial soap. Aren't you glad you have him? Don't you wish everybody did?
- God is like...the U.S. Post Office. Neither rain, nor snow, nor sleet, nor ice will keep him from his appointed destination.
- God is like...Frosted Flakes. He's greeeeeaaaaaatttt!

Potential comparisons are all around you and can help you think about old situations in new ways. Next time you are frustrated, take a walk around your home, office, or meeting room and the grounds surrounding that place. Look for objects, situations, or events that you can compare with the subject. For example, maybe you are looking for ways to communicate better with your volunteer team. You walk around the parking lot and notice a pothole. How is your difficulty in communicating with your volunteer team like a pothole?

SLEEP ON IT

Sleep is one of my favorite catalysts. No kidding—sleeping will help you be more creative. No one is sure why sleep is so important to life. You might think your brain rests while you sleep, but studies show that while the rest of the body is catching a few z's, neurons in our brains are firing away furiously throughout most of the night. The only time your brain really rests (and even then it is still active) is when you are in the deepest part of sleep, called non-REM sleep, which makes up about 20 percent of your total sleep cycle.

Scientists still don't know exactly how much sleep each individual needs. Sleep schedules change with age and with gender. Puberty and pregnancy affect sleep needs. But scientists do know that we become dysfunctional with too little sleep—and also with too much sleep. You need to determine the amount of sleep that's right for you.

> "One NASA study showed that a 26-minute nap improved a pilot's performance by more than 34 percent."
>
> JOHN MEDINA, *BRAIN RULES*

As we age, we tend to get less sleep and some evidence suggests we need less sleep. Teenagers need more sleep—especially in the morning—so it's best for youth workers to avoid starting classes before 9:00 a.m.

Lyndon Baines Johnson, the 36th president of the United States, used to take a 30-minute mid-afternoon nap. The practice of a siesta is common in many cultures. Our bodies need these breaks. As a public speaker I know the worst time to be scheduled to speak or lead a workshop is in the mid afternoon. More traffic accidents happen during the mid-afternoon than at any other time of the day.

As we sleep we replay certain daily learning experiences. We need to shut off the exterior world for a period of time. We are learning as we sleep. One function of sleep may be to consolidate memories. Long-term storage of memory seems to undergo a conversion of some kind over weeks and months as our memories, facts, and experiences are gradually transferred from an initial storage area in the hippocampus to a more permanent place in the cortex.

The point is that dreaming and meditation provide opportunities for subconscious thought that can stimulate creativity. Removed from conscious attention, the brain does not stop, but ideas begin to associate randomly. They

**CATALYSTS
FOR CREATIVITY**

become unshackled from the forces of logic, convention, and habit that normally prevent the uninhibited linking of thoughts and information. This gives an idea time to incubate. Dreams are a rich source of ideas. Dreams reveal things you did not know you knew.

Researchers have noted that creative innovation often occurs during sleep or other periods of diminished arousal. However contemporary thinking suggests that sleep takes existing creative ideas and then modifies, redefines, and transforms them into original and innovative concepts.

> "The effects of sleep deprivation are thought to cost U.S. businesses more than $100 billion a year."
>
> JOHN MEDINA, *BRAIN RULES*

Balzac, the great French novelist, once said that he liked to work first thing in the morning so he could take advantage of the fact that his brain worked while he slept. He liked to get up and act immediately on the brain work that had been happening overnight.

When asked where he found his melodies, Johann Sebastian Bach said the problem was not finding them; it was getting up in the morning and not stepping on them. Thomas Edison sometimes slept on a table in his laboratory so he could start work as soon as he woke up and not forget any new ideas he'd come up with during the night.

Elias Howe secured the patent for the sewing machine (beating out Isaac Singer) based on an idea that came to him in a dream. Howe reportedly dreamed of being captured by savages who carried spears with holes in the tips. Upon awakening, Howe realized he should put the hole for the thread at the end of the needle, not the top or middle. This minor modification made the sewing machine a reality.

In 1921 German scientist Otto Loewi came up with an experiment that lead to the discovery of the neurotransmitter, which is what neurons use to communicate with one another. Loewi said it was in a dream that he came up with the idea of an experiment with frogs that would demonstrate the chemical, rather than electrical, nature of nervous impulse transmission. In fact, he actually had *three* dreams about a neurotransmitter. After the first one, he awoke briefly but went right back to sleep—and then could not remember the details in the morning. On another night he dreamt again, and this time he wrote some notes on a piece of paper. But in the morning he found he could not read his handwriting. Fortunately, for him he had the dream a third time—and this time he woke up and went right to his laboratory and did the experiment. He won the Nobel Prize in Physiology or Medicine in 1936 for his work.

Loewi wasn't the only one to find creative inspiration in a dream. Here are just a few others:

- Robert Louis Stevenson said the plot for *Dr. Jekyll and Mr. Hyde* came in a dream.
- Physicist Niels Bohr conceived of a model of the atom in a dream.
- Dmitri Mendeleyev dreamed the solution for the arrangement of the Periodic Table of the Elements.
- Samuel Taylor Coleridge dreamed the poem "Kubla Khan" before he wrote it.

Psychologists have demonstrated that the human brain is only able to retain a few chunks of information at a time. As mentioned earlier in this book, after a few seconds recall is poor, and after a few minutes the information will disappear entirely unless you repeat the information to yourself or write it down.

You may want to keep a notebook by your bed so you can record details from your dreams immediately after waking up, while they are fresh in your mind. Also consider keeping a small memo pad next to the shower, and a bound journal with you at all times. Also consider using a tape recorder.

Leonardo da Vinci's technique for getting ideas was to close his eyes, relax totally, and cover a sheet of paper with random lines and scribbles. He would then open his eyes and look for images and patterns, objects, faces, or events in the scribble. Many of his inventions came forth unbeckoned from this random scribbling.

In the last few years my best ideas have come on cross-country flights with my iPod playing my favorite songs in a relaxed almost sleep mode. Ideas just seem to float to the surface. I've read that when Einstein was troubled by a problem, he used to lie down and take a long nap. Now that is my kind of creative genius!

CATALYSTS FOR CREATIVITY

HOLY DISCONTENT

You might be surprised to hear that creative ideas sometimes grow out of irritation, like the pearl that grows around an irritating grain of sand inside an oyster's shell. Sometimes our dissatisfaction over the way things are is the creative catalyst that inspires a new vision for what could be.

Author Bill Hybels refers to such dissatisfaction or irritation as "holy discontent"—and I believe it can be a tremendous catalyst for creativity. There are probably one or two things in this world that you just can't stand. Maybe it's some kind of injustice that causes your blood to boil and the veins to pop out on your forehead. Maybe it's some situation that when you read or hear about it, you want to make a poster and march up and down the city streets trying to make a difference. Such discontent is the soil in which seeds of change are often planted.

"So how do you know what your Holy Discontent is? Whatever your answer, your one thing will move you off dead center, get you off the couch, and thrust you into the game, where its fight, fight, fight until some progress starts to show up! Once you say yes to serving God's agenda in the world, he then begins the process of channeling the holy-discontent frustration into a positive vision that propels you into a future charged with energy and purpose. At some point along the way, you'll find yourself so astounded by the kingdom-oriented voltage coursing through your veins that you'll lift up your head and with no inhibition whatsoever shout, 'I was born for this!'"

BILL HYBELS, *HOLY DISCONTENT*

Often we think of Jesus as a man who was never angry, a guy who sat around reading stories to children and carrying a lamb in his arms. But think about the different moments when Jesus was fuming with holy discontent. Like the moment he walked into his Father's house and saw people using it as a flea market. Jesus turned over the tables, yelled at people, and made a complete mess of everything. Part of discovering our passion comes when we discover and pay attention to the things that bring us that kind of holy discontent.

AWAKENING YOUR CREATIVITY

SO-NOT-DONE QUESTIONS

1. Do you think extrinsic motivation is ever legitimate? If yes, in what situations?

2. What colors are on the walls of your youth room? Is it an inviting room that entices you to come in? If not, how can you improve them?

3. How can you make your meetings more playful and fun?

4. On a creativity scale of 1-10 (10 being best), how does your youth room and office rate?

5. What do you see on your drive to work?

6. List several ways Jesus compares/describes himself (example: The Good Shepherd), and what do those images mean?

7. What current problem or opportunity are you facing, and what might you compare it to?

8. What ticks you off?

9. What's the one thing that gives you the most passion and energy? How would you complete the following statement: "I was born to_____."

TAPPING INTO YOUR TEAM'S CREATIVITY

CHAPTER SIX

In this chapter I want to introduce you to some proven creative techniques that work in bringing out the creativity among both your adult volunteer team and your student leaders. Some of these strategies will be familiar to you, but I'll offer you some ways of making them more effective. Others may be new to you, and I hope you're game to give them a try.

But the effectiveness of just about any technique you use will depend on the attitudes of you and your team members. I have found that leaders of creative volunteer and student teams:

- Respect opinions and encourage their expressions
- Encourage curiosity
- Express appreciation and praise for attempts at creativity
- Derive pleasure from being with the team
- Ask what the team thinks and feels
- Explain reasons for procedures
- Support members to think in new ways

If your work is grounded in these attitudes, your team is sure to be more creative.

TEN ICEBREAKER IDEAS TO GET YOUR TEAM GOING:

1. Have each person give their best and worst moments from the previous week.

2. Have everyone name something that makes them different from anyone else in the group.

3. Have each person make three statements about themselves, two true statements and one lie. See if others can guess which statement in false.

4. Get to know you questions:

   - What do you do for fun?

   - What quality do you appreciate most in a friend?

   - What is one characteristic you received from your parents that you want to keep?

   - What is one characteristic you received from your parents that you wish you could change?

   - What is one good thing happening in your life right now?

   - What would you like people to say at your funeral?

   - When, if ever, did God become more then a word to you? How did that happen?

5. Draw a timeline to chart the major events of your life.

6. Imagine your house is on fire. What five things would you rescue (besides people and animals)?

7. What three things would you take to a deserted island?

8. Name two people (past or present) you admire and why.

9. Play twenty questions.

10. Play "I spy…"

MAKING MEETINGS MATTER

Meetings are not my first love. In fact, you might even say I have a real aversion to meetings. I know I'm not alone in this. So why do so many of us hate meetings? Well, let me offer a few of my reasons. I tend to loathe most meetings because…

- My plate is full with other responsibilities

- My time is valuable

- Most meetings are boring

- They do not meet my needs
- They are not practical
- There is no agenda
- Nothing gets accomplished

I think we've all been to meetings that match that description. But let's flip the question around: What makes for a good meeting? For me, meetings are worthwhile when...

- They are practical
- Something does get accomplished
- They are fun and captivating
- They are relational
- They involve everyone
- They inspire me
- I learn something new
- They encourage creative thinking

BRAINSTORMING THAT WORKS

Back in 1941, Alex Osborne, an advertising executive in Buffalo, New York, formalized brainstorming as a systematic effort and disciplined practice to produce ideas in a group. Osborne's idea was to create an uninhibited environment that would encourage imaginative ideas and thoughts and defer critical judgment until later.

Osborne believed that bringing a team of people together to toss out suggestions in an environment free of judgment would lead to twice as many creative ideas than those same individuals might produce on their own. But is that true? Are most brainstorming sessions truly effective? A lot of research says they are not. In a famous 1987 report, researchers Michael Diehl and Wolfgang Stroebe from Tubingen University in Germany looked at 25 different experiments done by psychologists all over the world and found that groups that met together in brainstorming sessions were never more productive than "virtual groups" of individuals all working on the same problem by themselves.

In fact, real groups that engaged in brainstorming consistently generated only about half the number of ideas those same people would have produced if group members had all pondered the problem individually.

Studies consistently show that individuals working alone come up with more and better ideas than they do when working in a group—and the larger the group, the greater the disparity. There are a number of reasons for this. In working with a group, people tend to feel self-consciousness and anxious about being evaluated by other group members. Plus it is difficult to listen simultaneously to others while creating one's own ideas. Evidence suggests that individuals do better alone because participants are free to focus on their own ideas and more ideas are generated compared to traditional brainstorming.

> "Brainstorming is a little like a group of people meeting to make a sculpture. Everyone brings a piece of clay to the meeting and places it on the table. The pieces are molded together into a core and then the sculpture is turned, re-arranged, modified, reduced, expanded, and otherwise changed until the group agrees on the final sculpture."
>
> MICHAEL MICHALKO, *TINKERTOYS*

> "In ancient Greece, Socrates and his friends so revered the concept of group dialogue that they bound themselves by principles of discussion that they established to maintain a sense of collegiality."
>
> MICHAEL MICHALKO, *CRACKING CREATIVITY*

If brainstorming teams are not as effective as individuals coming up with ideas alone, why would I suggest it as a way of generating more creativity? I continue to encourage brainstorming because it is a very common form of team interaction and, with some small changes, it can still be helpful in tapping into a team's creativity. I want you to be aware not only of the limitations of brainstorming but also of the latest and most valuable tips and tricks of the trade that will enhance your experience and help your team to be far more productive.

When brainstorming works, it involves true dialogue. In Greek, the word *dialogue* means a "talking through." The Greeks believed the key to establishing dialogue is to exchange ideas without trying to change someone's mind. This is not the same as *discussion*, which from its Latin root means to "dash to pieces." The basic rules of dialogue for the Greeks were: "Don't argue," "don't interrupt," and "listen carefully." That is immensely practical advice for brainstorming sessions. Here are some more basic suggestions to make brainstorming work:

- Invite people from diverse areas.

- The larger the brainstorming group, the fewer ideas produced. The ideal number of participants is between six and eight.

- Participants should have a positive attitude and be fluent and flexible thinkers.

- Participants should be strong, independent personalities.

- Discourage observers, onlookers, and guests.

- Have a written, flexible agenda.

- Select a location that is comfortable, private, and away from your normal meeting place.

- The group leader should have strong interpersonal skills and be able to paraphrase and find analogies for suggestions.

- The group leader should frame the problem as clearly and specifically as possible, but refrain from indicating a preferred solution.

- All participants must regard each other as equal colleagues.

- Rotate membership and bring in "new blood" as tasks change.

- Encourage any and all ideas, the more bizarre the better.

- Participants should build on one another's ideas, allowing suggestions to bounce of one another to trigger additional ideas and combinations of ideas, multiplying the possibilities.

- Protect dissenters by publicly supporting them.

Remember, brainstorming is not critical thinking. Effective brainstorming demands that we delay all judgment and criticism. Participants should not judge or evaluate ideas as they are generated. Nothing kills creativity more quickly or more absolutely than critical, judgmental statements.

No idea is a bad idea. Now, you may be thinking, "Well, I have met some bad ideas in my time"—and I have, too. But I am saying that no idea is a bad idea especially when brainstorming, because even the worst suggestion may trigger someone else to share a brilliant idea. That brilliant idea would never have been spoken if the previous idea had not been shared. All creativity stops when someone in the brainstorming group shares an idea and someone else says, "Yes, but...." You must have a "no but" rule. Instead of saying "Yes, but..." people can say "Yes, and...." Instead of contradicting one another's

ideas, we add to what others have said—a technique known as plussing, piggy-backing, or hitchhiking.

Withhold all evaluation of ideas until the end of the session. At the end of a brainstorming meeting, review and evaluate all suggestions making two lists: "Ideas of Immediate Usefulness" and "Areas for Further Exploration."

Here are a couple more ideas to make your group's brainstorming more productive:

- Before the group meets, schedule 15-20 minutes for members to brainstorm individually. I recommend a mixture of group and individual work to maximize your creativity.

- One way of enlivening your brainstorming is to consider how your group could create the opposite of what you really want. Take a goal, reverse it, and then talk about what you would do to achieve the reversed goal. For example, if your goal is to make attending youth group as desirable as possible, you've probably considered the question of how you'd do that many times. But what would happen if you reversed the goal? What would you do to make the students' experience as horrible as possible? How could you drive students *away*? The answers might yield some interesting and unique insights.

- If you can't get your group together in person, try online brainstorming (members type ideas into their computers, and the ideas appear on other participants' screens).

A study done by J. Hall and W. Watson reported that groups that were given the following instructions were judged to be more creative and superior to groups who did not receive these instructions 75 percent of the time.

- Avoid changing your mind only in order to avoid conflict and to reach agreement and harmony.

- Withstand pressures to yield which have no objective or logically sound foundation.

- View differences of opinion as both natural and helpful.

DOROTHY LEONARD AND WALTER SWAP, *WHEN SPARKS FLY*

STORYBOARDING

Storyboarding is a team activity credited to Walt Disney. Back in 1928, when Walt Disney and his artists were working on his first talking cartoon, "Steamboat Willie," Disney wanted full animation. To animate everything required thousands of drawings, which were piled in stacks all over the place. It was hard to know what had been finished and what still needed to be done. They had to have meetings all the time just to stay up to date with what was going on.

Walt Disney came up with the idea of having his artists pin their drawings on the walls of the studio in sequence so everyone could see how far along the project was. Each scene was a point around which a complete story could be told—hence the term *storyboarding*.

Storyboarding quickly became a routine part of Disney's planning procedure for both animated and live-action films. He could walk in at any time of the day or night and see progress on any given project at a glance. He also began using storyboard planning for projects beyond films. Both Disneyland and Walt Disney World were operationally planned using storyboards. At times, Disney would have up to 2,000 cards on walls throughout the building.

Although Walt Disney is credited with the modern technique of story boarding, Leonardo da Vinci used to pin his own ideas up on a wall and examine them over time. This visual display of ideas enabled him to see how one idea related to another and how all the pieces came together.

Storyboarding has been refined over the years into workable procedures for generating and developing all kinds of ideas and projects. Although there are some significant differences among the different processes, all of them share the common feature of laying out key concepts in a way that they are linked together to form a complete whole.

You can use storyboarding to lay out your thoughts and the thoughts of others as you work on your problem or opportunity. You can use a wide variety of materials to create your storyboard: Corkboards, white boards, chalkboards, walls—anything that provides a surface upon which you can add, delete, or move things around. You can use different colors to distinguish headers and columns. Depending on which system you use, you may need pushpins, scissors, marking pens, chalk, 3x5 cards, sticky notes, or other types of paper.

To get a feel for how you might use storyboarding, let's look at how you might use it as part of the planning process for a summer camp:

- Gather the planning group (6-8 people) around a table where they can all see the board you'll be using. You want the board to be something people can see from a distance. You will also need a couple hundred blank 3x5 cards scattered on the table, with markers for people to use.

- Create a topic card that says "PLANNING SUMMER CAMP" and place it on the upper left hand corner of the corkboard using a push pin. You want to put the pin at the top of the card, just to the left of the center.

- Ask participants what major categories need to be considered for summer camp. As the team members offer suggestions like "food," "location," "games," "speakers," "sound equipment," "music," or "transportation," have the person making each suggestion write it on a 3x5 card, bring the card up to the cork board, and pin it to the board directly below the topic card. The physical act of writing the topics and getting out of their chairs and walking up to put the cards on the board gets the blood moving in the legs and is stimulating to the mind. Some people will love just being able to get out of their chairs and move around. Also, with the movement in the room and people saying their ideas one after the other, inhibitions will begin to melt away and people will be more likely to share ideas. (As with brainstorming, there are no bad ideas—no suggestions should be evaluated or criticized at this point.)

- Once you have all the categories on the corkboard (there could be dozens of cards on the board), take one of the cards on the corkboard, (for example, "food") and move it to the top of the board where it can become a topic card. Then start the process again, asking for specific food suggestions for camp. Participants may come up with suggestions like "tacos," "sloppy Joes," "hamburgers," "hot dogs," and "pizza"—and again, each of these is written on a card and put on the corkboard.

- Once all the food possibilities are on the board, take one of the food cards and make it a topic card. And start the process again. For example, under the "taco" card, people might list ingredients like "meat," "lettuce," "beans," "guacamole," etc.

TAPPING INTO YOUR TEAM'S CREATIVITY

- Repeat this process with each item from your original categories for planning your summer camp. Fine tune the list as you break it down into smaller units. You could end up with hundreds of cards on the corkboard.

- You can stop the process at any time and come back to it on another day. If you do stop the process, take a roll of transparent tape and starting at the top of each list, run the tape down the center of each group of cards (that's why you put the push pin just to the left of center of each 3x5 card). Then take out all the pushpins, and you can fold the list of taped cards up like an accordion and save them for another day. Or if you finish the process, you can hand one the folded sets of cards (such as the set of ingredients in the taco meal) to an individual who will be responsible for getting the tacos to the camp. You might also take a photograph of the board so it can be reconstructed and reworked in the future, if necessary.

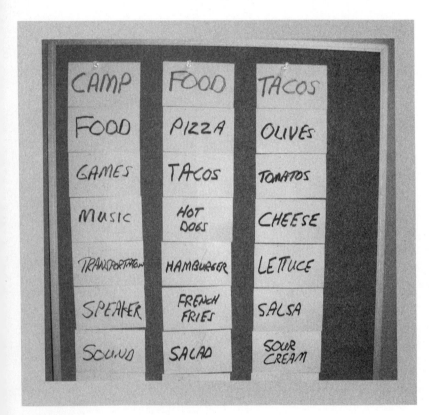

REAL DEADLINES

Deadlines can stimulate creativity—or they can hinder it. There is a general belief that people tend to generate their best ideas when time is tight and deadlines are looming. However, in one of the most comprehensive and ambitious attempts ever made at understanding creativity in action, Harvard Business School professor and leading creativity researcher Teresa Amabile showed this to be a myth. Her study found that people tended to be less creative when working under serious time pressures.

However, the study found some instances in which time pressure did inspire creativity among some people. That occurred when the person was fully focused and the deadlines were real.

In short, a real deadline may concentrate the mind, at least in some cases. But artificial deadlines can kill originality. The best strategy is to work on projects long before they are due. This requires time management.

DEVIL'S ADVOCATE

To stimulate your team's creative juices, it may be helpful sometimes to play the role of devil's advocate. The term comes from the Roman Catholic tradition; the "devil's advocate" is an official of the Congregation of Rites whose duty is to point out defects in the evidence upon which the case for beatification or canonization rests.

In a team setting, a devil's advocate takes the opposite view from others in the group in order to push people and get them thinking. When this technique is used to create ideas in a team setting, the devil's advocate should be a good role player. Other participants should not know the person's actual position, or the questioning will not be taken seriously.

"Walt Disney allowed his vivid imagination to produce fantastic ideas, uncritically and unrestrained. Later, he engineered these fantasies into feasible ideas and then evaluated them. To evaluate them, he would shift his perspective three times by playing three separate and distinct roles: The dreamer, the realist, and the critic.

"On the first day, he would play the dreamer and dream up fantasies and wishful visions. He would let his imagination soar without worrying about how to implement his conceptions. His fantasy analogies permitted him to connect words, concepts, and ideas with apparently irrelevant objects and events. The result was a rich treasure of associations; an imagination avalanche with whole mountains of ideas crashing down.

"The next day, he would try to bring his fantasies back to earth by playing the realist. As a realist, he would look for ways to engineer his ideas into something workable and practical.

"Finally, on the last day, he would play the part of the critic and poke holes into his ideas."

MICHAEL MICHALKO, *TINKERTOYS*

I don't recommend using the devil's advocate strategy early in a discussion, as it might stifle creativity. But as ideas are being refined, this technique of taking the opposite view can be helpful. I would only use this method occasionally—maybe a couple of times a year at most. And I would avoid having the same person be the devil's advocate each time.

This can be a wonderful method to get people thinking creatively when your students keep parroting back the answers they think you want to hear

in a Bible study. Challenge their thinking and shake them up. You may even want to consider inviting a friend the students do not know come into a Bible study and challenge what you are teaching your students. It will shock your students at first, but then you should give the students the opportunity to answer this stranger's questions and concerns.

WHAT IF?

I love to ask groups to do the creative mental exercise that involves asking the question "what if?" This activity can also be done individually, but I find more ideas are generated when it is done in a team setting. It is a great way to learn to direct your imagination toward a desired goal.

I have written a series of five quick question books designed to get conversations going with teenagers. One of my books is called *What If...?* It contains 450 thought-provoking "what if" questions designed to spark lively discussions, vigorous debates, and creative thinking. You can use this same concept to tap into the creativity that is within your team.

"What if"-ing can be used to take the brainstorming process one step backward. In other words, before you tackle a real-life problem or issue, ask some fun "what if" questions just to get people talking and thinking. The process acts as a right-brain lubricant that can stimulate weird ideas without the possibility of judgment. Try some of these:

- What if you inherited five million dollars?
- What if you could pick any superhero's powers?
- What if you could eat anything and not get fat?
- What if you could make yourself invisible?
- What if you could read people's minds?
- What if you could ask God three questions?

Another good way to stretch your team's imagination is to ask "what if" someone else were solving your problem or opportunity. How would Spider-man, the custodian of your building, your aunt, Mother Teresa, Bill Gates, a five-year-old child, or Steven Spielberg answer your question?

And what about Jesus? Do you remember the WWJD bracelets? (I always thought WWJD stood for "Who Would Jesus Date?") The question "What Would Jesus Do?" is still a good one to ask in any situation.

GROWING CIRCLES

Growing circles is an innovative and unusual exercise to get the minds of your team members thinking. Sometimes called "mind mapping," this technique was developed in the early 1970s by Tony Buzan, a British brain researcher. It's an organized brainstorming method that helps people discover what they know by depicting thoughts and associations as vines growing in all directions from a central word or theme. The associations are potentially infinite, as each new association can trigger others.

Suppose you are in charge of planning the upcoming Easter program for your ministry. You could just sit down with your team and ask what they want to do for Easter. Or you could try growing circles. You'd begin that process by writing the word Easter in the center of a piece of paper and drawing a circle or oval around it. Then draw lines going out from the circle. At then end of each line, put whatever words or phrases come to the minds of your team when they think of Easter. Now circle those words, and draw lines coming out from those newly circled words. What do you think of when you see and hear those words? Write those thoughts down and circle them.

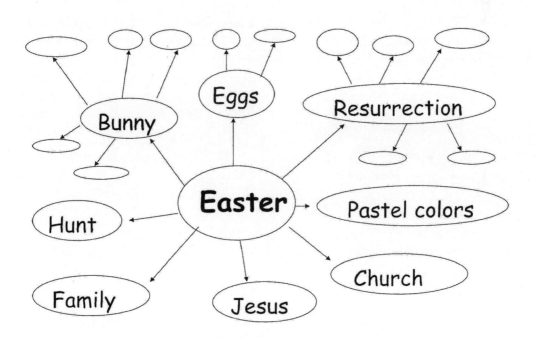

TAPPING INTO YOUR TEAM'S CREATIVITY

You can keep going and going as far out as you would like. You'll end up with a whole lot of words and phrases that all began with the word Easter. Now you can use these words and phrases as springboards as you plan skits, talks, publicity, set decorations, worship experiences, and games on the subject of Easter. You can also try this exercise by beginning with a word or phrase describing a problem or possibility in your ministry.

MICRO MOVEMENTS

The concept of micro movements was developed by observing how doctors helped patients who were partially paralyzed. Instead of trying to gain movement of an entire arm, they would focus patients on one small movement, like moving one finger a fraction of an inch. By having success with smaller achievements, they hope to make progress toward larger goals.

The same idea is used in psychiatry. Patients are encouraged to take small strides towards recovery. Do you remember the 1991 movie *What About Bob*? featuring Bill Murray as a patient and Richard Dreyfuss as a psychiatrist? The doctor urged his patient to take "baby steps"—to overcome his fears and phobias in small increments.

One way I use this technique in a team-building creativity session is by having participants write down on a 3x5 card some creative desire, idea, or dream they have had for their ministry or their life. Maybe it's an item on their "bucket list"—something they hope to do before they die, or "kick the bucket." Some examples might include:

- Sail a boat to Tahiti
- Be a ballerina
- Paint a painting
- Sing a song in public
- Sky dive
- Heal a relationship
- Fly a plane
- Read the entire Bible
- Write a book

I then have each person take another 3x5 card and list all the reasons why they can't accomplish this vision, desire, idea, or dream. I tell them they'll be the only one to see the card, so they can just list words, phrases, or fragmented thoughts. I then have them read over all the reasons they've listed about why their dream is impossible. Then I have them take that card with all those reasons and excuses and tear it into pieces, and throw the torn-up card into a trash can I provide. It's important to have people get these negative ideas on paper and look at them. I don't want them to be in the backs of their minds or they will never accomplish their dream. They have to get these thoughts out of their head and onto a piece of paper and then let go of the belief that these things can stop them form accomplishing their dreams. As Hebrews 12:1 urges, "Let us strip off everything that slows us down and hinders us" (NLT).

I then have them take their original 3x5 card with the thing they want to accomplish and write one small step, one micro movement, that they can take toward realizing that dream. The task should be something very small, something that will take them no more than an hour. But it would get them started on the journey. It could be to look up something about the subject on the Internet or at a library. It could be visiting a store or making a phone call.

> "Go confidently in the direction of your dreams! Live the life you imagined."
>
> THOREAU

But they're still not done. I now have them all write on the 3x5 card the date and time (within one week) when they will take this tiny step toward their individual goals. And then I encourage them to tell someone what they are going to do, because we are all more likely to do a task if we've told someone else. I conclude the session by inviting those who are willing to tell the rest of our team their dream and the micro movement they've decided to make.

As the old saying goes: "Inch by inch, life's a cinch—but yard by yard, it's miles too hard." Small successes are stepping-stones to greater ones—in ministry and in life.

We all act, feel, and perform in accordance with what we imagine to be true about ourselves and our environment. What you imagine to be

true becomes, in fact, true. If you hold a certain picture of yourself in your mind's eye long enough and steadily enough, you will become that picture. Imagine yourself achieving your goal and that alone will contribute immeasurably to success.

My greatest fear for the members of my ministry team is that they'll end their lives with a feeling of emptiness. They'll look back on a life full of coulda, woulda, shouldas. Don't let this happen to you or your team or your ministry. Go for it. What do you have to lose?

> "You have a masterpiece inside you, too, you know. One unlike any that has ever been created, or ever will be. And remember: If you go to your grave without painting your masterpiece, it will not get painted. No one else can paint it. Only you."
>
> GORDON RAY MACKENZIE, *ORBITING THE GIANT HAIRBALL*

SO-NOT-DONE QUESTIONS

1. Describe your experiences in brainstorming.

2. Which ideas seem most feasible to you and your team?

3. Try this with your team the next time you meet. Pick a program you need some ideas on and put it on 3X5 cards and try storyboarding.

4. Where are you on the time continuum? Do you like to get things done far ahead of time? Just in the nick of time? Or after the deadline was due? Are you good with how this is working for you? If not what can you do?

5. Have a friend come to your meeting and challenge what you are teaching your students. This may shock your students but it may also get them thinking in new ways as they attempt to answer the friends concerns.

6. What is your one dream, desire before you die? What is stopping you from doing it?

AWAKENING YOUR CREATIVITY

LIVING
CONCLUSION
IN THE LIGHT

The 17th century Dutch painter Rembrandt was a master of using light in his paintings. Rembrandt didn't just employ light and shadows to create drama and texture in his work. For him, light was central to the composition of the entire painting. Rembrandt's use of light gave his subjects a physical presence that fully involved the viewer.

Rembrandt was a believer, and in his religious paintings he sought to capture the living light of God. When Rembrandt depicted the Christ, Jesus himself was the source of light in those paintings. One of his last paintings was *The Prodigal Son*, which depicts the world-weary sinful son who had spent all his wealth in wasteful living returning home to the presence of his father.

Two centuries later another Dutch painter, Vincent Van Gogh, made creative use of light in his own work. One of Van Gogh's most famous paintings, Starry Night, depicts a night sky alight with blazing stars and swirling clouds. Like Rembrandt, Van Gogh used light to represent God in many of his paintings. He was a dedicated Christian with a strong and enthusiastic faith. He worked as an apprentice lay preacher and wanted to devote his life to the evangelization of the poor. In 1878, he began a three-month course in preaching in the Evangelist school in Laeken, near Brussels. Some leaders of the school believed Van Gogh was unsuitable for the preaching profession. But he persisted, going to the Belgian coal mining area close to the French border. There, living in extreme poverty, he visited sick people and read the Bible to the miners.

In 1879 he got permission to work as a lay preacher in Borinage. But his involvement in the plight of the poor irritated his superiors, and his contract was not extended. He continued to work without any pay until July 1880.

In Borinage, Vincent experienced a period of deep personal crisis, partly because of his negative experience with the church leaders. Van Gogh had so much to give to the world and the church, but his gifts were rejected.

Tragically, Vincent Van Gogh took his own life in 1890 at the age of 37. One of his final paintings was "The Church at Auvers."

Used with permission of the Museum d'Orsay, Paris, and the Van Gogh Museum, Amsterdam

I had a chance to see the original of this painting in Paris at the Museum d'Orsay. If you look carefully, you will see that there is no light (representing God) emanating from the church. There are also no doors—no way into the church. Van Gogh was one of the most creative minds of his or any time—a man who'd been eager to preach the gospel and serve the poor in God's name. Yet near the end of his life, the church was no longer a place of safety, refuge, and solace. It was a place of impending doom and gloom.

Van Gogh's story is an important reminder to those of us in youth ministry. We must never turn away a student or youth leader because he or she does not fit the mold. Instead, our youth ministries must free students and youth leaders to discover and express their God-given creativity.

The goal of being creative in youth ministry is to create a church in which the doors are wide open and kids have opportunities to experience the light. The bottom line of all these creative techniques is to help you build a ministry where kids experience God's love. Our task is to walk alongside students and help them experience the love of the One who created them, and then to help them find ways to creatively express that love to the world. In the end, that's what both creativity and youth ministry are all about.

Don McLean wrote his song "Vincent (Starry Starry Night)" in 1971 after reading a book about the life of Vincent Van Gogh. The song has become even more well known recently thanks to a rendition by Josh Groban and its being performed by contestants on *American Idol*. The final verse is poignant:

> For they could not love you
>
> but still your love was true,
>
> and when no hope was left in sight,
>
> on that starry starry night,
>
> you took your life as lovers often do.
>
> But I could have told you, Vincent,
>
> this world was never meant for one
>
> as beautiful as you.

LIVING
IN THE
LIGHT

BONUS SECTION

MORE CREATIVE IDEAS YOU CAN USE IMMEDIATELY IN YOUR YOUTH MINISTRY

The final section of this book includes a wide range of creative suggestions you can put to use in your youth ministry right now. These resources were developed by a lot of fine people I've come to know during my years in youth ministry. I have indicated the author and original source for the information wherever possible. Many of these lists were reprinted or adapted from handouts and presentations at various youth worker events sponsored by Youth Specialties over the years—including CORE and National Youth Workers Seminars—and supplemented by various workshop notes, conversations with other youth workers, and my own experiences in youth ministry. I am very grateful to the following creative men and women who have been a part of those YS seminar teams who have influenced my life and whose work can be seen on the following pages.

Dave Ambrose	Mark Helsel	Mark Matlock	Denny Rydberg
Denny Bellesi	Dave Hicks	Bill McNabb	Charley Scandlyn
Scott Burks	Megan Hutchinson	Brock Morgan	Efrem Smith
Jim Burns	Dan Jessup	Helen Musick	Sheryl Shaw
Ridge Burns	Ray Johnston	***Mark Oestreicher	Jeanne Stevens
Chap Clark	Crystal Kirgiss	Marv Penner	Becky Tirabassi
Doug Fields	Danny Kwon	Laurie Polich	Rich Van Pelt
Heather Flies	**Tic Long	Mark Rayburn	*Mike Yaconelli
Mike Giarrita	Fred Lynch	*Wayne Rice	
John Hall	Steve Mabry	Duffy Robbins	

I'm grateful to all the youth workers whose creative ideas are mixed in among these suggestions—including those who are specifically credited as well as others who remain unnamed. I hope you'll find these suggestions helpful as you seek to infuse your ministry with greater creativity.

* Cofounders of Youth Specialties
** former President of Events at Youth Specialties
*** President of Youth Specialties

CREATIVE WAYS TO BUILD ENVIRONMENTS CONDUCIVE TO LEARNING

Consider these factors as you seek to create environments that will best foster learning among your students:

- *Temperature*. Rooms too hot or too cold can make students simply incapable of concentrating on anything except the heat or chill. You remember in high school when late spring afternoons turned classrooms into ovens? Ideas don't need that kind of incubation.

- *Distractions*. A chattering toddler is a wonderful thing—but not in a Bible study. Arrange space with an ear as well an eye to the environment. How about light? You need enough to read by, but warm atmospheres aren't known for lots of it.

- *Seating*. Make it comfortable, and arrange it so that everyone can be easily seen and heard. Even Jesus chose boats and hillsides to teach from; he stood up when reading the Torah in synagogues. If comfort must be compromised, let it be the teacher who endures. Outdoors, for example, if the sun must be in someone's eyes, let it be the teacher's.

- *Room selection.* It should suit the size of the group. Nothing makes a small group feel smaller than meeting in too large a room. And stuffing a big group into a modest living room is great for a Young Life club meeting, but it's probably not the best for study of the Scriptures.

- *Fatigue*. Tired students do not learn well. Nor, at 8:20 p.m., do anxious students who thought the study ended at 8 p.m. They will tune out, thinking more about tonight's homework and tomorrow's game than about your Sermon on the Mount study.

Source: *Teaching the Bible Creatively: How to Awaken Your Kids to Scripture* by Bill McNabb & Steven Mabry

BONUS SECTION

Curious about how your group perceives Jesus Christ? Want them to grasp some of the implications of being a Christian today? Ask the group to respond to the questions below as if they were each Jesus Christ here and now. Emphasize that there are no right or wrong answers; the main thing is that all respond based on how they think Christ would respond if he were alive today.

- What kind of clothes do you wear? Do you identify with any particular class of people (poor, middle class, upper class, a minority group, etc.)?

- Describe your family relationships—with your mother, father, brothers, and sisters. Do you have a girlfriend? Will you marry?

- What kind of people do you hang around with? What do you talk about?

- What do you look like?

- Where do you spend most of your time? What is your favorite hangout?

- Are you a controversial figure? Why or why not?

- How do you feel about the church today? How do you get along with the religious leaders today?

- How do you feel about the way things are in this country?

- What are your goals for the next years?

- How would you get your message out to as many people as possible? (Think this one through carefully, Jesus—are you sure the mass media is the best way to get your message across?)

- Where do you stand politically? Are you a party member? If so, of which party? What would you consider the important issues—unemployment, inflation, poverty, abortion, equality, environment, capitalism, military spending, nuclear proliferation?

After everyone has answered the questions individually, discuss them with the entire group. To move the discussion from the hypothetical to the actual, ask whether we Christians should respond to those questions in the same manner as our imagined, modern-day Christ. Aren't we to follow Christ and to pattern our lives after his example?

Source: *Teaching the Bible Creatively: How to Awaken Your Kids to Scripture* By Bill McNabb & Steven Mabry

CREATIVE WAYS TO HELP STUDENTS DEVELOP SPIRITUALLY THROUGH DISCOMFORT

We can encourage students to grow spiritually by urging them to...

- Confess a selfish act to a family member.
- Share a personal struggle with the youth group.
- Write an encouraging letter to the pastor.
- Volunteer to help a needy family in the church.
- Teach a Sunday school or youth group lesson.
- Commit to tutoring a younger student who is less privileged.
- Participate in a 30-hour famine (World Vision, 800-7-FAMINE).
- Give a Bible to a non-believing friend.
- Attend another church's worship services.
- Sponsor a kid through Compassion International (800-336-7676).
- Go backpacking, white-water rafting, or mountain biking.
- Volunteer to clean the sanctuary once a month for a year.
- Make an encouraging video for a missionary.
- Write cards to visitors and thank them for coming to church.
- Invite in spokespersons from other faiths, traditions, and denominations.
- Get to know one elderly couple, and listen to their story.
- Visit the biggest city near you and talk to strangers in the park.
- Pray for one non-friend at school every day for one semester.
- Organize a reconciliation group at school.
- Give away all of your paycheck to the poor for a month.
- Organize a baby-sit-for-free group for single parents.
- Send an encouraging letter to a parent of a friend.
- Offer to meet with the pastoral staff to discuss the needs of the kids.
- Set up a juvenile peer-counseling ministry.
- Put on a play at church.
- Gather toys for a children's hospital or orphanage.
- Skip a meal, then send the money they would have spent for the meal to a mission organization.
- Raise money for the homeless.
- Volunteer to help a needy family in the church.
- Visit a convalescent home.

Source: *Youth Specialties CORE Seminar Notebook*

BONUS SECTION

CREATIVE METHODS TO COMMUNICATE YOUR MESSAGE

Your talks will be more creative if you add:

- Chalkboard/Whiteboard
- Maps
- DVD
- PowerPoint
- Monologue
- Symposium
- Student teachers

Your group discussion will be more creative if you include:

- Brainstorming
- Buzz groups
- Circle response
- Question/answer
- Debate
- Panels
- Problem solving
- Quizzes
- Forums
- Listening teams
- Book reports
- Interviews
- Open ended sentences
- Character comparisons
- Word associations

Try these other creative ways to communicate your message...

- Role playing
- Collages
- Dioramas
- Field trips
- Choral speaking
- Character interviews
- Mobiles
- Puppets
- Pantomime
- Litanies
- Murals
- Rebuses
- Time lines
- Triptychs
- Opinions
- Research assignments
- Diaries
- Newspaper headlines
- Letter writings
- Spontaneous dramas
- Maps
- Paraphrases
- Commercials
- Prayers
- Emotional graphs
- Posters
- Use of clay, dough, pipe cleaners, and other creative media
- Raps
- Cheers
- Poetry
- Painting (finger, sponge, string, sand)

Source: *Youth Specialties National Resource Seminar Notebook*

AWAKENING YOUR CREATIVITY

CREATIVE WAYS TO
MOTIVATE TEENS TO LEARN

- Kids learn better when they experience.

- Kids learn better in a comfortable environment.

- Kids learn better when they discuss what they are learning.

- Kids are motivated to learn when the answer is not obvious.

- Kids learn better when the focus is on the concrete.

- Kids learn better when they help to choose what they study.

- Kids learn better when they can translate terms into their own language.

- Kids learn better when they are challenged to be creative.

- Kids learn better in varied settings.

- Kids learn better under the guidance of a mentor.

- Kids learn more when their lessons affect their lives.

BONUS SECTION

Source: *Teaching the Bible Creatively: How to Awaken Your Kids to Scripture* By Bill McNabb & Steven Mabry

- Have the church send off the youth group every time they leave for a mission trip, camp, or retreat.

- Develop a blessing service for young people graduating and going to college.

- Have young people contribute in meaningful ways to every worship service.

- Get adults praying for specific kids on a regular basis.

- Once a year have adults plan a mystery day or weekend for the teens.

- Develop small groups of young people who surprise elderly members of the church by showing up to their houses and doing yard work or miscellaneous repairs.

- At finals time have adults in the church tutor kids.

- Provide a study hall for the week before exams complete with music, food, and computers.

- Develop partners (one adult with one young person) to email weekly.

- Partner young people with adults to do a service project.

AWAKENING
YOUR CREATIVITY

Source: *Youth Specialties National Resource Seminar Notebook*

CREATIVE WAYS TO
GET TO KNOW YOUR KIDS

- Go to sports events.
- Read school newspapers.
- Check out the high school yearbook.
- Get an F.B.I. background check.
- Interview a baby-sitter.
- Talk to parents.
- Visit their rooms.
  - o Check out the bulletin boards.
  - o Look at books, magazines, CDs.
  - o Observe posters and pictures.
- Read a teen magazine.
- Visit their school at lunch.
- Interview school personnel (teachers, counselors, principal, janitor).
- Ask them what music they like.
- Ask them what hobbies they like.
- Notice their clothing style.
- Hang out at the mall or local gathering place.

BONUS SECTION

Source: *Youth Specialties National Resource Seminar Notebook*

137

- Write a letter to God.

- Write a prayer of confession.

- Identify three action steps they will take to apply your next message.

- After reading Scripture, have each young person share with one other person what difference the content will make in his or her life.

- Write a prayer of thanksgiving.

- Send a letter to a parent.

- Clean up the youth room.

- Help design the youth group's bulletin board with ideas that reflect a recent sermon message or study topic.

- List friends they can pray for and invite to church.

- Volunteer their time in the children's ministry, nursery, etc.

- Design a greeting team to care for visitors.

- Make greeting cards that reflect the theme or message of a recent event and send them to students who missed the event.

- Organize a prayer group.

- Write a letter to a missionary.

- Write a plan for becoming missionaries on their own campuses.

- Develop a hunger bank.

- Give a Bible to a friend.

- Encourage a friend.

- Adopt a grandparent within the church.

Source: *Youth Specialties National Resource Seminar Notebook*

GETTING KIDS STARTED (REALISTIC, SPECIFIC GOAL)

- Canned food drive
- Free car wash
- Free babysitting
- Food scavenger hunt
- Paint church at 3 a.m. as part of a fun lock-in
- One day of work for city "graffiti crew"
- Flowers to shut-ins on Mother's/Father's Day
- Parents' appreciation night

EVENTS REQUIRING DEEPER COMMITMENT

- Christmas in July for senior citizens in convalescent home
- Thanksgiving food drive for needy
- Get kids on church boards
- Secondhand repair shop
- Trips to the inner city
- Trips out of the country
- Ministry to prisoners

OTHER IDEAS:

Share the Warmth
Collect blankets, jackets, and mittens for needy kids or the homeless in your community. Make the exercise even more meaningful by having the youth group do the distribution.

Multiplied Money
Teach from the parable of the talents in Luke 19 and then give each of your students $5 (or a pair of students $10) and challenge them to make money with what they've been given over the period of a week or two. Use the money to provide hunger relief or aid some other worthy community cause.

Complete Christmas

Instead of just collecting toys to be given out to children in need at Christmas, invite your group to take on a family and provide a complete Christmas. Let students take responsibility for the different components of the family Christmas as individuals or in groups—a few could get together and buy the tree, a few more could split the cost of the turkey, and someone else could buy cranberry sauce or vegetables.

Farm Aid

Instead of doing a missions trip to the inner city, find a small, rural community and work with the local church to do ministry projects with farm families who would appreciate the help—one family a day for a week.

Spring Camp Preparation

Find a camp or nonprofit summer ministry that needs help getting things ready for their seasonal program. Many camps will let youth groups have a whole weekend on their site if they are willing to put in a full Saturday of work. Fall clean-up is an equally good idea.

VBS/Day Camp Program

Train a few of your key students as children's workers and find a community where you can provide a Vacation Bible School or day camp program. Work with a local Christian family to host your students and provide the on-site coordination.

Hospital Calls

Make and deliver poster-size get-well cards for church members and acquaintances in the hospital. Spend 10 minutes or so with the patient, putting the poster on the wall, chatting, and praying together. If you can, give a bouquet of balloons as well.

Source: *Youth Specialties National Resource Seminar Notebook*

Celebrate the commitment you see in your youth group by giving these awards to kids who qualify. Please note that each of these awards can be presented to more than one person. You may have several students who fit the criteria for some of these honors—and it might be nice to give every kid an award.

Andrew Award
- For a kid who consistently brings friends to youth group or introduces them to the Lord. (John 1:42)

Simon Peter Award
- For a passionate kid who steps out boldly and takes risks in his faith journey. (Matthew 14:29)

Barnabas Award
- For a kid who is always encouraging other students and leaders in the group. (Acts 4:36)

Timothy Award
- For a kid who is an example of spiritual discipline. (1 Timothy 4:12)

Aaron Award
- For a kid who works faithfully behind the scenes in a significant support role. (Exodus 4:15)

Esther Award
- For a girl who shows courage. (Esther)

You may be able to think of other Bible-based awards for students who embody positive traits seen in other biblical characters. But you'll probably want to avoid these...

Delilah Award
- For the girl most likely to cause the boys in your group to abandon their convictions.

Enoch Award
- For the kid in your group you wish would just disappear.

BONUS SECTION

Source: *Youth Specialties National Resource Seminars*

Body-Art Award
- For the volunteer with the most piercings and tattoos.

Too-Old-to-Quit-Now Award
- For the oldest volunteer on your team.

Trying-Not-to-Look-My-Age Award
- For the volunteer who most looks younger than he or she is (have the group vote if there are several candidates).

ER Award
- For the volunteer who most recently had to call an ambulance to an event or take a kid to the emergency room.

Roadside-Assistance Award
- For the volunteer with the most (or most recent) bus or church-van towings.

Still-Hanging-in-There Award
- For the volunteer who's been at it the longest.

Enron-Financial-Management Award
- For the volunteer who lost the most money on a fundraiser.

Or these other ideas:

Big-Trouble Award
- For a volunteer who has done something really dumb.

Foot-in-the-Mouth Award
- For a volunteer who has said something that got him or her in some deep trouble.

Overachiever Award
- For the volunteer who puts in more hours than the others combined.

Early-Bird Award
- For the volunteer who is always on-time—and usually early.

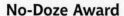

No-Doze Award

- For the volunteer who's always the most energetic at a lock-in or overnighter.

Best-Supporting-Role Award

- For a faithful spouse who isn't involved in frontline ministry but makes it easy for his or her partner to be involved.

The Diamond Prayer

One Word: A seemingly impossible situation you've faced

_____

Two Words: Adjectives that describe the situation

_____   _____

Three Words: About you or an action you took

_____   _____   _____

Four Words: About what you wanted to happen

_____   _____   _____   _____

GOD POURS OUT HIS SPIRIT

Four Words: About God, or an action he took
marking the turning point for the better

_____   _____   _____   _____

Three Words: About you or an action you took

_____   _____   _____

Two Words: Adjectives that describe the situation or
how you felt about the situation

_____   _____

One Word: The opposite of the word used at the top

_____

EXAMPLE: This was written by a woman who struggled with infertility for years:

INFERTILITY

HOPELESS/SAD

CRIED/PRAYED/HOPED

BABY/LOVE/ARMS FILLED/LIFE FILLED

GOD POURS OUT HIS SPIRIT

ADOPTION/#1/#2/#3

NATHAN/LAURA/WILL

OVERJOYED/COMPLETE

MOMMY

Source: Youth Specialties CORE Seminar Notebook, 2004

Learn names.
- Take individual photos of students in your group, mount each picture on a piece of cardstock, and write the student's name under the picture. Put the cards up in the youth room. When students bring friends, do the same for these guests. This will help you and the kids remember names.

Acknowledge birthdays.
- Send students funny or encouraging birthday cards. You don't have to spend a lot of money on birthday cards; send birthday greetings on something unusual, like an airline barf bag, or use the Internet to send a card online. Have the youth group sing an appropriate song to students born during the month. Call kids on or before their birthdays.

Listen to their stories.
- Once or twice a month allow a student one minute to share how she met Christ. Or hold an interview segment during the youth meeting when you interview a teen chosen at random about his week or about the best thing that happened recently. You could also film students in groups of two or three, telling about their most embarrassing moments or funniest memories together.

Ask for their opinions.
- Do periodic surveys to get student feedback and adult leadership input about possible activities, topics for study, and other changes that might be made. Surveys can be done informally, through casual—though purposeful—conversations, or through more formal methods, like prepared surveys. For example, give students a blank piece of paper and ask them to write down four topics they'd like to see the group study, three activities they'd like to see the group do, two ways to make the youth group better, and one way they could be better used or involved in the ministry.

Help them become experts at something.
- Whether it's helping students refine their existing interests or inspiring them to try something that you do well, helping kids develop special skills is a great way to connect with them. Even something as simple as throwing passes to a budding football player or hitting ground balls to a shortstop gives you an instant connection. Think about some area of expertise you might

AWAKENING YOUR CREATIVITY

have—Web design, music, photography, sports, cooking, art, interior design, skiing, etc., and look for ways to pass your skills along.

Wake up call.

- Have the video camera running as you sneak into a student's room early some morning—with a parent's cooperation, of course. Use the brass section of the marching band, a foghorn, a gas-powered leaf blower, or a bucket of water as the alarm and catch the fun on tape.

Look who's coming to dinner.

- Invite students over for dinner. Let students sign up for dinner parties in groups of three or four. That allows them to come along with some friends they already know, and makes them feel a lot more relaxed around your table. Put the names of each dinner group in a hat, and have a drawing once a month. The winning group gets some home cookin' at your place. It saves you from figuring out who's comfortable with whom, and it also allows the kids to do the work of organizing a group. All you have to do is give them a date and you're on!

Set up intergenerational prayer partners.

- This is a great way to get the older members of your church involved in your youth ministry. Some adults may not want to spend time with junior highers, but they may be willing to pray for them. Furnish pictures of students along with some pertinent facts. Include some specific prayer requests from the students.

Go to their events.

- This is not reserved for the big football game. How about an oboe recital or a chess competition? This is also a good way meet their peers. Send them a brief note of encouragement after the event.

Send encouraging email notes and Internet cards.

- Kids love to get mail, and it's so easy with the Internet. You can send a quick note of encouragement or a funny card just to say, "Hi."

Source: *Youth Specialties National Resource Seminar Notebook*

BONUS SECTION

I have given you the framework for the lesson with the object, Scripture, and theme/focus:

Alka-Seltzer and 7UP
Ephesians 4:26-27, 31-32
Fuming in the Heart & Foaming at the Mouth

Band-Aids, Ace bandages, butterfly bandages (plus other kinds and sizes)
Psalm 32:5; 1 John 1:9
Cleansing, Closing, and Confessing

Blue cheese (and other substances with intense, distinctive odors, such as deodorant, cologne or perfume, scented candles, spoiled food, etc.)
2 Corinthians 2:14-15
Your Nose Knows

Canes, crutches, walkers
Psalm 37:23-24; 1 Peter 5:6-7
Lean on God

Coffin
Luke 12:16-26; Matthew 6:19-21
Cramming for the Final

Coloring book
Numbers 14; Romans 12:1-2
Coloring Outside the Lines

Feet, photos of
Psalm 40:1-2; Psalm 56:13; Isaiah 52:7
Beautiful Feet

Glove
John 15:5-6; Galatians 2:20
Letting God Give Us a Hand

Keys (many kinds, and a lock that one of the keys opens)
John 14:6; Acts 4:12
One Key

Large Rocks (in sturdy bag)
Hebrews 12:1-3; Philippians 3:12-14
What's Weighing You Down?

Mirror (hand-held)
James 1:22-25
Reflecting On the Reflection

Mousetrap (and cheese)
1 Corinthians 10:13; James 1:13-19
Traps

Piñata (and candy)
Romans 8:18-38; 2 Corinthians 4:7-12
The Surprises of Brokenness

Popsicle sticks
James 3:3-5
Say "Ahhhhh"

Shoes (all styles, sizes, colors)
Micah 6:8, Colossians 2:6-7
If the Shoe Fits

Water (preferably lake, but swimming pool, baptismal font, washtub, etc., will do)
Exodus 20:5-6; Galatians 5:7-9
Ripple Effect

Source: *Everyday Object Lessons for Youth Groups* by Helen Musick and Duffy Robbins

BONUS SECTION

I have given you the framework for the lesson with the location, Scripture, and theme:

Jail
Acts 16:16-36
To come close to experiencing Paul and Silas experience in prison.

Dump
Matthew 6:19-24
Invest your energy in things that last forever rather than things that crumble and rot.

Construction Pit
Genesis 37
A graphic identification with the experience of young Joseph.

Tower
Luke 4:1-13; 1 Corinthians 10:11-13
Getting a better idea of the temptation of Christ.

Boat
Matthew 14:22-32
Put complete trust in Christ no matter the circumstances.

Athletic Track
Hebrews 12:1-3; 1 Corinthians 9:24-27
Running the race of life for Christ.

Rooftop
Mark 2:1-12
No obstacle is too great to bring your friends to Jesus.

Garden
Matthew 26:36-46
God suffered in our place.

Cemetery
Psalm 103:14-16; Isaiah 25:3; Luke 20: 34-38; 1 Thessalonians 4:13
The reality of death and the promise of eternal life.

Tree
Luke 19:1-10
Jesus comes to us while we are still sinners.

Courtroom
Malachi 3:5; Acts 17:31; Romans 2:2-16; 2 Peter 2:9
God is a just judge.

Lighthouse
Matthew 5:14-16
Christians must let others see Christ by their actions and words.

Bank Vault
Mark 10:17-27
We should invest our treasure in permanent things.

Vineyard
John 15:1-17
We must stick to Christ in order for our lives to bear fruit.

Nursing Home
Job 12:12; Proverbs 16:31; Psalm 92:12-15
Old people have great worth, value, and wisdom.

Nursery
Mark 10:15; Matthew 18:2-6
We must have the faith of a child.

Beach
John 21
Reenact Christ's breakfast on the beach.

Source: Rick Bundschuh, *On-Site: 40 On-Location Youth Programs*

The All-You-Can't-Eat Fundraising Dinner

You can sponsor a successful money-making dinner by not holding one at all. That's right! Ask people to contribute a set amount for the dinner, but tell them they don't have to bother attending. Because there is no dinner and donors know this, you are freed from the organizational hassle of putting together a successful dinner or banquet. The only work you need to do is sell tickets, which you would have had to do anyway if you actually held the dinner.

You can finance a complete retreat, for example, if each young person who wants to attend sells enough tickets to pay his or her way. For example, if your winter retreat will cost $75 per person and your tickets to your non-event sell for $5, each retreat participant can pay his or her way by selling 15 tickets.

You can create a ribbon memento of the non-event by using thicker stock paper on your church or organization photocopy machine. Everyone who purchases a ticket gets a ribbon. Ribbons help people remember the all-you-can't-eat dinner, and why they gave to it.

Free Car Wash

Set up a youth-sponsored car wash at a local shopping center or filling station as you normally would. However, instead of charging for the wash tickets, give them away. Advertise is as a "FREE CAR WASH." Make it clear that there are no strings attached. Anyone may get their car washed free by the youth of your church as a gesture of Christian love and friendship. Those who wish to make a contribution can do so using any amount they choose. Post a sign at the car wash site similar to this one:

Your car is being washed by the youth of First Church. This is a free service with no strings attached. It's a small way for us to demonstrate to you the love of Jesus Christ.

Another way we are attempting to share Christ's love is by collecting funds to help purchase food for people in need. If you would like to help us with this project, your contribution would be greatly appreciated. Thank you and God bless you.

Print this information on your tickets as well. One youth group did this twice and raised a total of $800. Pick a good day and a good (busy) location, make sure you have plenty of hardworking, friendly young people, and the experience can be very rewarding.

Kidnap the Pastor

Have the group "kidnap" the pastor and/or other well-known individuals in the church (prearranged, of course!) with the ransom being a set amount of money to be used for a youth project. This works best if done on a Saturday. Young people telephone members of the congregation informing them of the kidnappings and the ransom amount required. Church members can pledge a dollar amount to be given on Sunday morning. If the ransom isn't paid, the youth should be prepared to handle the morning service or the responsibilities of the other kidnapped individuals. Your group will have a ball being creative with this one.

Pledge-a-Thons

Pledge-a-Thons are popular fundraisers. Their popularity makes it easy to sign up sponsors who pledge money for every mile, hour, event, or other measurement. You can net thousands of dollars with a well-organized event. People generally are more willing to pledge when they know up front what their total commitment will be. Have your group members estimate the total pledge when they sign up their sponsors. Here are a few specific examples…

- **Lawn-a-Thon.** This is a unique way to raise money for your group. Line up as many young people as you can and provide lawn mowers and transportation for each of them. Advertise with flyers and posters that on a certain Saturday, your group will mow lawns for free! Get as many people as you can to sign up to have their lawn mowed. Have supporters pledge a certain amount for each lawn that is mowed.

- **Memorize-a-Thon.** Here's a fundraising "a-thon" that has spiritual benefits for your group as well as financial ones. Have a Bible Verse Memorize-a-thon where your youth get pledges for every Bible verse they learn. It's a contest that many people in your church will be eager to support.

- **Rock-a-Thon.** A 24-hour "Rock-a-Thon" involves everyone in the group and serves as a great fundraiser. Each participant signs up sponsors who pledge a certain amount for every hour the participant rocks in a rocking chair. Here are the rules:

  1. Everyone provides his or her own rocking chair.
  2. Each participant must rock at least four successive hours.
  3. Time breaks are allowed only for trips to the bathroom.
  4. The chair must be moving at all times.

- **Work-a-Thon.** The idea is to arrange jobs for the young people in elderly people's homes. The jobs could include painting, gardening, housekeeping, shopping, or any other service the kids could perform. Top priority should go to people from the church or community who cannot afford to pay for the work they need done. The young people then get donors to sponsor them for their work. On the arranged day, the young people work an eight-hour day at the different homes, free of charge to the people they are serving.

Source: David & Kathy Lynn, Great Fund Raising Ideas for Youth Groups

Every year our youth group traveled with a few other groups to Mexico to build houses for the poor. One of the youth groups we traveled with was from Beverly Hills, a very expensive place to live. As part of its annual fundraising to pay for the house, the Beverly Hills youth group sponsored an auction. Because it was located in Beverly Hills, this was no ordinary auction. People were asked to donate expensive items, and they did. One year the Beverly Hills youth group's fundraising goal was $22,000. One student was determined to raise the most money for the auction. He was bright, direct, a bit nerdy, and not intimidated by adults. We'll call him Henry.

Henry walked into the most exclusive bank in Beverly Hills and asked for the president. After giving him the coldest of stares, the receptionist sent Henry to the bank president's secretary. Unfazed, he asked, "Could I talk to the president for a few minutes?"

Barely acknowledging his presence, the secretary said, "He's busy. Very busy."

"That's okay," Henry said, "I've got the rest of the day. I'll wait." He waited for a couple of hours before the secretary came to Henry in a huff: "He said he has two minutes, but he's very busy."

As Henry walked into the president's massive and intimidating office, the president looked the boy up and down and said in a slightly irritated voice, "What can I do for you?"

"Well, I'm from Hollywood High School, and I – "

The president interrupted, "Hollywood High School? I graduated from there. Is Miss Granville still there and still a miss?"

"Uh, actually, she is."

"How about that? Well, what can I do for you, son? I imagine you're raising money for something. Will $100 do?"

"Actually I was wondering if the bank owned a condo."

Taken aback, the president responded warily, "Yes, we do."

"I was wondering if you would be willing to give us one week at your condo to auction in order to raise money to build houses for the poor in Mexico."

The bank president was so impressed, he said yes and determined which week the condo would be available.

As the boy was leaving, the bank president said, "By the way, can you accept cash?"

"Sure," Henry said confidently. The bank president sat down, wrote a check, and handed it to Henry. It was for $3,000.

Most kids would have been blown away and run back to the church to celebrate the good news. Not Henry. He was on a mission. Walking down the street to the next bank he could find, he entered and asked for the president. When the president finally met with him, Henry said, "We're raising money to build houses for the poor in Mexico. The bank down the street gave us $3,000. What are you going to do?" He walked out that bank with a check for $1,000.

In one afternoon Henry raised $4,000 in cash and a week at a condo that was auctioned for $2,000. Henry was creative. His ingenuity and courage had taken the bank presidents by surprise, and they responded. Henry didn't do fundraising the way it had always been done, and as a result, six families in Mexico now have homes of their own.

Source: Mike Yaconelli, *Youth Specialties National Resource Seminar Notebook*

BIBLIOGRAPHY

Aamondt, Sandra and Sam Wong. *Welcome to Your Brain.* New York: Bloomsbury, 2008.

Barker, Joel Arthur, *Future Edge.* Scranton, PA: William Morrow, 1992.

Bennis, Warren and Patricia Ward Biederman. *Organizing Genius: The Secrets of Creative Collaboration.* Reading, Massachusetts: Addison-Wesley, 1997.

Block, J. Richard and Harold Yuker. *Can You Believe Your Eyes?* New York: Gardner Press, 1989.

Brandreth, Gyles. *Optical Illusions.* New York: Sterling, 2003.

Bundschuh, Rick, *On Site: 40 On-Location Youth Programs.* Grand Rapids: Zondervan, 1989.

Christie, Les. *Best-Ever Games for Youth Ministry.* Loveland, CO: Group, 2005.

De Bono, Edward. *Serious Creativity: Using the Power of Lateral Thinking to Create New Ideas.* New York: HarperCollins, 1992.

Hall, Doug and David Wrecker. *Jump Start Your Brain.* New York: Warner Books, 1995.

Johansson, Frans. *The Medici Effect: What Elephants and Epidemics Can Teach Us about Innovation.* Boston: Harvard Business School Press, 2006.

LeFever, Marlene D. *Creative Teaching Methods.* Elgin, Illinois: David C. Cook, 1985.

Leonard, Dorothy A. and Walter C. Swap. *When Sparks Fly: Harnessing the Power of Group Creativity. Boston:* Harvard Business School Press, 1999.

Losey, John. *Experiential Youth Ministry Handbook + Volume II: Using Intentional Activity to Grow the Whole Person.* Grand Rapids: Zondervan, 2007.

Lynn, David & Kathy. *Great Fund Raising Ideas for Youth Groups.* Grand Rapids: Zondervan, 1993.

MacKenzie, Gordon. *Orbiting the Giant Hairball: A Corporate Fool's Guide to Surviving with Grace.* New York: Viking Penguin, 1998.

McNabb, Bill and Steven Mabry. *Teaching the Bible Creatively.* Grand Rapids: Zondervan, 1990.

Medina, John. *Brain Rules.* Seattle: Pear Press, 2008.

Michalko, Michael. *Cracking Creativity: The Secrets of Creative Genius.* Berkeley, CA: Ten Speed Press, 2001.

Michalko, Michael. Thinkertoys: *A Handbook of Creative-Thinking Techniques,* 2nd ed. Berkeley, CA: Ten Speed Press, 2006.

Musick, Helen and Duffy Robbins. *Everyday Object Lessons for Youth Groups,* Grand Rapids, Zondervan, 1999.

Pink, Daniel H. *A Whole New Mind: Why Right-Brainers Will Rule the Future.* New York: Riverhead, 2005.

Putzier, John. *Get Weird! 101 Innovative Ways to Make Your Company a Great Place to Work.* New York: AMACOM American Management Association, 2001.

Rowe, Alan J. *Creative Intelligence: Discovering the Innovative Potential in Ourselves and Others.* Upper Saddle River, NJ: Pearson Education, Inc., 2004.

Ruggiero, Vincent Ryan. *Becoming a Critical Thinker,* 6th ed. Boston: Houghton Mifflin, 2009.

Sarcone, Gianni and Marie-Jo Waeber. *Eye Tricks: Visual Deceptions and Brain Teasers.* London: Carlton Books, 2007.

Schramm, Dr. Derek D., Ph.D. *The Creative Brain.* Institute for Natural Resources: Health Update, Home-Study #2290, December 2007.

Schultz, Thom and Joani. *Why Nobody Learns Much of Anything at Church: And How to Fix It.* Loveland, CO: Group, 1993.

Von Oech, Roger. *A Whack on the Side of the Head: How You Can Be More Creative.* New York: Warner Books, 1990.

Von Oech, Roger. *A Kick in the Seat of the Pants: Using Your Explorer, Artist, Judge & Warrior to be More Creative.* New York: Harper & Row, 1986.

Walford, Rosie with Paula Benson and Paul West. *Shelf Life.* New York: Bloomsbury Publishing, 2004.

White, Jeff. *Holy Wow: Boost Your Youth Ministry Creativity.* Loveland, CO: Group, 2004.

Yaconelli, Mike. *The CORE Realities of Youth Ministry.* Grand Rapids: Zondervan, 2003.

CREDITS

Selections from Doug Hall, *Jump Start Your Brain*, reprinted with permission of Eureka! Ranch Technology, 1995.

Selections from Gordon Ray MacKenzie, *Orbiting the Giant Hairball* (Used by permission of Viking Penguin, a division of Penguin Group (USA) Inc., copyright © 1996).

Selections from Edward de Bono, *Serious Creativity: Using the Power of Lateral Thinking to Create New Ideas* (Reprinted with permission of HarperCollins.)

Selections from Michael Michalko, *Tinkertoys* (Copyright 2006 by Michael Michalko, Ten Speed Press, Berkeley, CA. www.tenspeed.com. Reprinted with permission.)

Selections from Michael Michalko, *Cracking Creativity* (Copyright 2001 by Michael Michalko, Ten Speed Press, Berkeley, CA. www.tenspeed.com. Reprinted with permission.)

Selections from *Brain Rules* by John Medina reprinted with permission of Pear Press.

Drawings from *Creative Teaching Methods* by Marlene D. LeFever reprinted with permission of David C. Cook Publishing.

Selections from Mary R. Schramm, *Gifts of Grace*. Reprinted with permission of Augsburg Publishing.

Selections from Jeff White, *Holy Wow* (Group Publishing, 2004) reprinted with the author's permission.

Selections from *The Medici Effect* by Frans Johansson, reprinted by permission of Harvard Business School Press, Boston, MA, 2006.

Selections for Warren Bennis, *Organizing Genius*, reprinted with permission of Basic Books, a member of Perseus Books Group, 1997.

Selections from *A Whack on the Side of the Head* by Roger von Oech reprinted with permission of Grand Central Publishing.

Selections from *Creative Intelligence: Discovering the Innovative Potential in Ourselves and Others*, by Alan J. Rowe. 1st ed., 2004. Reprinted by permission of Pearson Education, Inc. Upper Saddle River, NJ.

Selections from *When Sparks Fly* by Dorothy Leonard and Walter Swap. Reprinted with permission from Harvard Business School Press 2005.

Selections from *Welcome to Your Brain*, Sandra Aamondt and Sam Wang, Reprinted with permission from Bloomsbury Publishing, 2008.

Selections from *The Core Realities of Youth Ministry* by Mike Yaconelli, *Great Fund Raising Ideas for Youth Groups* by David & Kathy Lynn, and *On Site: 40 On-Location Youth Programs* by Rick Bundschuh all reprinted with permission of Zondervan.

QUICK QUESTIONS BOOKS BY LES CHRISTIE
What If...

Have You Ever...

Gimme Five...

Unfinished Sentences

The Little Book of Worsts

OTHER BOOKS BY LES CHRISTIE
When Church Kids Go Bad: How to Love and Work with Rude, Obnoxious, and Apathetic Students

Best-Ever Games for Youth Ministry

AWAKENING YOUR CREATIVITY

LOST iN SPACE

everything you wanted to know

about planets, stars, galaxies, and beyond

BY **MEGAN GENDELL**

WITH **RACHEL CONNOLLY,** SPACE EDUCATOR
CONSULTANT

SCHOLASTIC INC.

New York • Toronto • London • Auckland • Sydney
Mexico City • New Delhi • Hong Kong • Buenos Aires

ISBN-10: 0-545-04455-3

ISBN-13: 978-0-545-04455-4

Designer: Lee Kaplan

Illustrations: Yancey Labat

Comic Story: Robin Lyon

Photos:

All photos provided by NASA unless otherwise noted.

Front cover: NASA/JPL–Caltech/N. Smith (Univ. of Colorado at Boulder)

Back cover: NASA, ESA, the Hubble Heritage Team (STScI/AURA) and J. Green (University of Colorado, Boulder)

Page 6: (quarter) George Allen Penton/Shutterstock.com; (North America) NASA/R. Stöckli/Robert Simmon/GSFC/MODIS.
Page 7: (Milky Way) NASA; (galaxy cluster) NASA, ESA, Richard Ellis (Caltech) and Jean-Paul Kneib (Observatoire Midi-Pyrenees, France); (string of galaxies) NASA. Pages 7, 14–15: (Earth) R. Stöckli/Robert Simmon/ NASA GSFC/MODIS; (Sun) SOHO (ESA & NASA); (Mercury) NASA/JPL; (Venus) PASA/Pioneer Venus; (Earth) R. Stöckli/Robert Simmon/ NASA GSFC/MODIS; (Mars) NASA/ STSCI/Colorado/Cornell/SS; (Jupiter) NASA/JPL/USGS; (Saturn) NASA/JPL; (Uranus) NASA/JPL; (Neptune) NASA/JPL. Page 8: (night sky) Dan70/Shutterstock.com. Page 9: (Stardust) NASA Kennedy Space Center (NASA–KSC); (Hubble) NASA; (Sputnik) NASA History Office; (Luna 3) NASA History Office. Page 10: (Earth) R. Stöckli/Robert Simmon/ NASA GSFC/MODIS; (astronaut) NASA. Page 13: (left) NASA/JPL–Caltech/J. Rho (SSC/Caltech); (right) NASA/JPL/University of Arizona. Page 14: (Pluto) Illustration: Thomas Nakid. Page 15: (blueberries) Wellford Tiller/Shutterstock.com; (grape) Yuli Amstislavski/Shutterstock.com; (basketball) Vincent Giordano/Shutterstock.com; (walnut) Mark Lijesen/Shutterstock.com. Page 16: (Io) NASA/JPL; (Europa) NASA. Page 17: (Miranda) NASA; (Titan) NASA; (Dactyl) NASA. Page 18: (Moon) NASA/SPL/USGS; (Far side of Moon) Apollo 16/NASA. Page 19: (Earth and Moon) NASA/JPL; (Galileo) North Wind Picture Archives. Page 20: NASA. Page 21: Illustration: NASA/JPL. Page 22: (binary stars) NASA/Tod Strohmayer (GSFC)/Dana Berry (Chandra X-Ray Observatory); (baby stars) NASA/JPL–Caltech/N. Smith (Univ. of Colorado at Boulder). Page 23: (supernova blast) NASA/J.J. Hester, Arizona State University; (black hole) Illustration: NASA/CXC/M.Weiss. Page 24: Hinode JAXA/NASA. Page 25: SOHO/ Extreme Ultraviolet Imaging Telescope (EIT) consortium. Page 26: Hubble Heritage Team (STScI) and NASA. Page 27: (Thor's Helmet Nebula) Canada–France–Hawaii Telescope/J.-C. Cuillandre/Coelum; (Butterfly Nebula) NASA/STScI; (Messier) Roger Viollet/Getty Images. Page 28: (spiral galaxy) NASA, Hubble Heritage Team, STScI, AURA; (elliptical galaxy) Jim Misti; (irregular galaxy) NASA/ESA/Hubble. Page 29: Jim Misti. Page 30: (barred spiral galaxy) Jim Misti; (Pinwheel Galaxy) NASA. Page 31: (Antennae Galaxies) NASA, ESA, and the Hubble Heritage Team (STScI/AURA)–ESA/ Hubble Collaboration; (Sombrero Galaxy) NASA/Hubble Heritage Team; (Tadpole Galaxy); (Halton Arp) Courtesy Dr. Halton Arp. Page 32: (ISS) NASA; (Earth) NASA.

For information regarding permission, write to Scholastic Inc., Attention: Permissions Department, 557 Broadway, New York, NY 10012.

SCHOLASTIC, THE ULTIMATE SPACE CLUB, and associated logos are trademarks and/or registered trademarks of Scholastic Inc.

12 11 10 9 8 7 6 5 4 3 2 1   7 8 9 10 11/0

Printed in the U.S.A.

First printing, November 2007

TABLE OF **contents**

Be sure to visit the **Ultimate Space Club**
online at: **http://www.scholastic.com/ultimatespace**
This month's secret password is: **goexplore**

MISSION: universe

WELCOME TO the universe. You've lived in it your whole life, and now you're about to learn all about it! What's out there beyond our planet, our sun, and the stars, moon, and planets you see in the sky each night? And what are all those stars, anyway?

There are a lot of things out in space—planets, stars, huge groups of stars called galaxies, and a whole lot of gas and dust. All of these things help make up the universe. The universe contains every single thing that we've ever observed—all the way down to you, your pets, and what you ate for breakfast this morning.

✴ It's a Big Wide World ✴

The universe is so big that we can't measure it in miles, like we measure distances on Earth. Instead, scientists measure distance in space in **light-years**. A light-year is the distance light can travel during a year. Light is the fastest thing we know. In a year, it travels almost 6 trillion miles—that's almost 6,000,000,000,000 miles! If you could go that fast, you could circle Earth seven times in a single second.

That means a light-year is a really, really long distance. The Sun might seem far away, but it's only a teeny-tiny fraction of a light-year from Earth. It takes light just eight minutes to get from the Sun to us! So, how many years

MEASURING UP

If you could reduce our solar system to the size of a quarter, the Milky Way would be as big as the United States!

Where Are YOU in the Universe?

Humans are very tiny specks compared to the enormous size of the universe. But that doesn't mean we don't know our way around this huge place! You live in a building that's part of a neighborhood, and your neighborhood is part of a city, and your city is part of a state. But it doesn't stop there. If you could keep zooming out, you'd see your country, then your continent, and then your entire planet. From there, it's time to move out into space! Here's what you'd find:

would it take light to get from one side of the universe to the other? Nobody knows for sure, but scientists think it would take 156 billion years. That's one big universe!

SCOTTY'S SPACE TRAVEL TIPS

Hi, it's me, Scotty! If you could travel 40,000 miles per hour, you could make it around Earth twice in about an hour. Going that fast, it would still take you 40,000,000,000 years to get to the nearest galaxy like our own! The universe hasn't even been around that many years!

What's Out There?

Anything you can imagine might exist somewhere out there in the universe. Pink elephants? Flying pigs? Machines that do your homework for you? Planets with purple skies and two suns? Aliens with six eyes and super-fast spaceships? You never know! Scientists have only explored a teeny-tiny portion of the universe.

In this book, you'll find out about some of the planets, moons, stars, and galaxies we've discovered so far. You can only imagine what we *haven't* discovered yet!

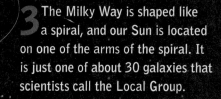

2 The Sun is at the center of our solar system. It's just one of billions of stars in a big group called the Milky Way Galaxy.

1 The planet you live on, Earth, is part of our solar system.

3 The Milky Way is shaped like a spiral, and our Sun is located on one of the arms of the spiral. It is just one of about 30 galaxies that scientists call the Local Group.

5 Scientists think **galaxy** clusters make up giant sheets and strings that spread across the universe. Our galaxy is part of the "Great Wall" of galaxies. This structure is still just one small part of the universe—but scientists are still learning about what exists beyond it!

4 The Local Group, together with many other groups of galaxies (like the Virgo Cluster, which includes 2,000 galaxies), makes up the Virgo Supercluster. Our supercluster is just one of millions of superclusters in the universe!

LET'S GO exploring!

IF YOU'VE got a brain full of questions, you're going to have a brain full of answers before you know it. Asking questions about the things around you and looking for the answers is what being a scientist is all about, and it's scientists who explore space.

Space Scientists

Different kinds of scientists look at different kinds of things. A scientist who explores the universe is called an **astronomer**. Astronomers can study all sorts of things: planets, stars, galaxies, special kinds of light, and lots more. Here are some special kinds of astronomers:

Astrophysicists study all kinds of objects in the universe, including how stars form and affect other objects.

Astrogeologists study how planets formed and what they're made of.

Astrobiologists study where in the universe life might be able to exist and how to search for it.

You've probably also heard about **astronauts**. Astronauts are scientists, pilots, and engineers who travel into space on rockets to work. They do science experiments, build space stations, fix satellites, and more!

How's Your Eyesight?

You can see far enough to read the blackboard at the front of your classroom, or to recognize your best friend from across the playground. You can even see planets, stars, and galaxies that are 2.5 million light-years away! But what if you wanted to learn about stars in other galaxies? Or planets that are orbiting other stars?

Stellar Tools

We explore the universe by looking out into space but you can only see so much light with your eyes. That's why astronomers have created all sorts of tools to travel out into space and gather more light. Huge telescopes on Earth can take photographs of galaxies that are far away.

Astronomers have also sent telescopes out into space, where they can see into the

BLORP'S Fun Facts

Blorp! Did you know that humans can't see most kinds of light? Only 2 percent of light is visible to the human eye. That's why people use telescopes to learn even more about the universe!

universe without having to look through Earth's atmosphere first.

Astronomers have also created cool robots, satellites, and space probes to travel into space and visit planets, moons, and other objects. These probes can do tests on the materials they find and sometimes even send stuff back to Earth. You'll find out about a bunch of cool space probes as you make your way through this book.

Clockwise from upper left: *Sputnik*, *Stardust*, *Hubble Space Telescope*, and *Luna 3*

Space Travel Teams

Many countries have their own organizations that send rockets, robots, people, and probes out into space. The U.S. government created NASA, the National Aeronautics and Space Administration, to be in charge of exploring space. Over the years they've sent people into space and sent probes to visit planets, moons, comets, asteroids, and even the Sun. There are many other countries that also have their own space agencies!

Clockwise from top: Logos for the space agencies of India, Russia, China, Japan, and the United States

In Your Space Kit

REMOTE CONTROL ROCKET LAUNCHER

Want to get a better idea of what launching all of these rockets and space probes is like? Get the Remote Control Rocket Launcher from your Space Kit and give it a try! It uses the air pressure that builds up from the reaction between vinegar and baking soda to send it flying into the air.

Don't forget to decorate your rocket using the stickers in your kit. And when you're all done, store your kit items in your rocket-shaped Space Collectibles Case for safekeeping!

WHEN YOU LOOK into the night sky, you can see a lot of stars. But what do you see in between all those stars? Just a lot of empty space, right? In fact, everything outside of the Earth's atmosphere (and the atmospheres of other planets and moons) is known as **space**. Space includes planets, moons, rocks, ice, gas, dust, and lots and *lots* of empty space.

The first thing humans ever sent into space was a satellite called *Sputnik*, which the Soviet Union sent to orbit Earth in 1957. A couple of years later, they sent the first spacecraft to the Moon, and people saw the far side of the Moon for the first time. The first human went into space in 1961, and by 1969, the first man had set foot on the Moon! Humans have been spending time out in space ever since, doing science experiments, taking photographs, and learning everything they can about our planet and the space around it.

MEASURING UP

If you could shrink Earth down to the size of a basketball, astronauts on the Space Shuttle would be orbiting Earth just a quarter of an inch (6 mm) from the surface. The Moon would be about 23 feet (7 m) away from the basketball. Suddenly the Moon doesn't seem so nearby, does it?

No Air out There!

In between the planets, moons, and other stuff out there, space is empty. Emptier than your stomach before breakfast. Emptier than a trash can after you take out the trash. Even emptier than your ice cream bowl after you've licked it clean.

How can anything be emptier than that? Space is missing one thing that every empty thing on Earth is full of: **air**. That means humans need to bring their own oxygen when they're out in space. This is also why space is black. On Earth, the air scatters the light from the Sun and gives us a blue sky. In space, there's nothing to reflect and scatter the light, so everything is black.

In Your Space Kit

SPACE SIMULATOR

What would happen if you went into space and all the air pressure on Earth went away? Grab the Space Simulator in your Space Kit and get ready to find out.

Your Space Simulator imitates the lack of air in space. So, what lucky object should you send up there? Start by putting a big, fresh marshmallow inside. Then pump the handle up and down a few times until it gets difficult. Pumping removes air from inside the Space Simulator. Just like space has no air, the inside of your Space Simulator now has less air, and also less air pressure.

As you do this, watch what happens to your marshmallow! Press the air release button and you'll really see the effect "space" had on the marshmallow. Now try putting some fizzy soda inside your Space Simulator. What happens to the bubbles in the soda?

Hey, No Pressure!

The air that makes up Earth's atmosphere constantly presses down on your body from all sides. You can't feel it because you're used to it. But out in space, no air means there's no pressure at all. What would that be like? Try out the Space Simulator in your Space Kit, and you'll see for yourself!

I Just Can't "Weight"

Out in space, everything's weightless. There's no up or down. There's no floor or ceiling. Astronauts fly around by pushing off the sides of their spacecraft, and they keep floating until they hit something else! Down on Earth, the planet's gravity keeps our feet on the ground (and when you jump, it brings you right back down).

Since everything floats onboard the Space Shuttle, you'll need to do things a little differently than you do down on Earth! You'll need straps for your feet to keep you in place, and deep pockets with flaps so your things don't fly away. And watch out—when you get hot, even your sweat will float off your skin!

If you went out into space without a space suit, your blood would turn bubbly just like the soda in your Space Simulator. That's why scientists developed space suits to keep pressure around our bodies when we go into space.

POP CULTURE

In the 2002 movie *Treasure Planet*, spaceships look like 15th-century sailing ships. Sure, they looked cool, but you don't want to be standing on the deck of a sailboat in space. Just look at what happened to your marshmallow!

FREEZE! Sit as still as you can. Now answer this question: Are you moving? As a matter of fact, you are! You aren't moving around on your own, but the planet you live on, Earth, is spinning and whizzing around the Sun. And you're along for the ride!

The path Earth makes around the Sun is called its **orbit**. And Earth is just one of eight planets that go around the Sun. These planets are huge, round balls of rock, gas, and ice. They go around the Sun like cars around a racetrack. Together, our Sun, the planets, and all the other chunks of rock and ice that orbit around the Sun make up our **solar system**.

What Makes a Planet?

Every single planet is different. Some are big, some are small, some are hot, some are cold, and they come in all different colors. So, what makes a chunk of rock or gas a **planet**? Three things:

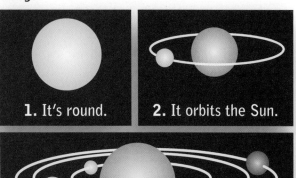

1. It's round.

2. It orbits the Sun.

3. It doesn't share its path around the Sun with any other objects (other than its own moons). So if a planet were a car on a racetrack, no other cars would be allowed on the same track as it.

Planets Far, Far Away

When you look into the night sky on a clear night, you can see hundreds of stars. Do any of them have their own planets orbiting around them? You bet! Scientists have discovered over 200 planets orbiting other stars and more are being discovered all the time.

The planets in other solar systems are probably a lot different from the planets that orbit our Sun. But they're so far away that we don't know much about them.

Could there be another planet out there like Earth? We know that none of the other planets in *our* solar system have the water *and* air that humans need to live. But not all life-forms need air to survive, and scientists think it's possible that there could be another planet with the water and energy for life to exist. That life could be in the form of bacteria that's so small it's invisible. Or it could be in the form of plants, trees, or even humans like us!

BLORP'S Fun Facts

Both Mars and one of the moons of Jupiter, Europa, have water. This might be the liquid water that's needed for life to exist! In 2007, scientists discovered an Earth-like planet called Gliese 581 c that has the right climate for liquid water and might be able to support life!

Stars forming in clouds of gas and dust

Where Do Baby Planets Come From?

You can't go shopping for planets at the mall.
Planets don't hatch from eggs. And planets
definitely don't grow on trees. So have the
planets in our solar system been around
forever? Nope! Like you, planets are born and
then grow up.

So how is a planet born? It all starts with
a swirling cloud of gas and dust. Everything
inside this cloud bumps and crashes around.
Then at the center, a star forms. That's when
things really start to heat up.

All around this star, bits of dust and gas
clump together and attract more and more
dust and gas from around them. As they get
bigger, they form into round balls. After a few
billion years, almost all of the dust and gas has
clumped together, and the balls have become
planets.

All the books, computers, ice cream, and
everything else around you came from a cloud
of gas and dust swirling around in space. That
means even *you* are made of stardust!

POP CULTURE

In the 2001 movie *Jimmy Neutron:
Boy Genius*, it takes just a few days
for Jimmy Neutron and his pals to fly
to planet Yolkus, in a far-off solar
system. But it would take us eight or
nine years just to get to Pluto, and it
could take tens of thousands of years
to make it to another solar system!

13

OUR SUPER SOLAR SYSTEM

YOU'VE SPENT your whole life on one planet. It has your family and friends, trees and beaches, and all of your favorite candy bars. This planet is called Earth, and it's the only planet in our solar system where you can find *any* of these things. But our solar system has seven other planets, in all different sizes and colors.

If you could weigh all the planets in our solar system, you'd find that **Jupiter** is heavier than all the other planets combined. That's a lot of gas!

Most planets spin upright, like tops, but **Uranus** spins on its side. Scientists think a giant rock the size of our planet knocked into it a long time ago and tipped it over.

Like Uranus, **Neptune** is a blue planet, because it's mostly made of a blue gas called methane.

Full of Cold Air

The outer half of our solar system is home to **Jupiter**, **Saturn**, **Uranus**, and **Neptune**. These planets are all called **gas giants**. They're much bigger than the first four planets, and they're made almost entirely of gas.

BLORP'S Fun Facts

Pluto used to be called a planet, but in 2006 scientists decided that since there were so many other big chunks of ice around it, Pluto was just another chunk, not an actual planet. But humans haven't forgotten about poor Pluto! A satellite called *New Horizons* is on its way to visit Pluto. It'll get there in 2015.

Mercury is the closest planet to the Sun, and it's so hot that parts of its rocky surface actually *melt* under the Sun.

Venus is covered in thick gas clouds around its surface that trap heat, like a blanket. This makes Venus even hotter than Mercury.

Earth is the cozy planet where you live, just the right distance from the Sun.

Mars is a chilly red planet that scientists think used to have water on its surface a long time ago!

Saturn is known by its giant set of rings, which are made of chunks of ice.

MEASURING UP

If you could shrink the Sun to the size of a basketball, how big would the other planets be by comparison? Check out this chart:

Mercury	poppy seed
Venus	poppy seed
Earth	peppercorn
Mars	peppercorn
Jupiter	walnut
Saturn	grape
Uranus	blueberry
Neptune	blueberry

MANY **moons**

YOU ALREADY KNOW that the big white disk you see in the sky most nights is really a giant hunk of rock that orbits around Earth. But did you know that our own Moon is just one of many moons out there, even within our own solar system? Some planets have two moons, and Jupiter has 60! (And more are being discovered all the time!) Can you imagine seeing two moons in the sky every night? How about a dozen moons?

Not all moons are gray like ours. Moons, like planets, come in all colors and sizes. And some scientists even think there could be life on other moons! Here are just a few of the amazing moons in our solar system. Just imagine the moons that might exist in the rest of the universe!

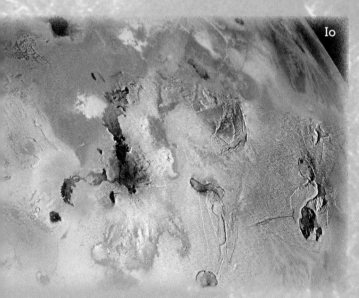

Io

IO

Io (usually pronounced EYE-oh) is one of Jupiter's moons, and it's covered in erupting volcanoes. Io is about the same size as our Moon, and it's about the same distance from Jupiter as our Moon is from Earth. But the similarities end there. The volcanoes on Io mean that the moon's surface is usually covered in pools of liquid sulfur. And while our Moon is covered in round craters from being hit by space rocks, the volcanoes on Io quickly fill up any craters that form.

EUROPA

Like Io, Europa orbits around Jupiter and is just a little bigger than our Moon. Unlike Io, Europa's surface is almost totally smooth, and it's covered with a layer of ice. The ice looks a lot like the ice that forms on Earth, except this ice is over 2 miles (3.2 km) thick! Scientists think there's liquid water under

Europa

the ice on Europa. In fact, there could be twice as much water on Europa as there is on Earth! For scientists, liquid water means there's the possibility for life to exist. If anything's there now, it's probably microscopic. But any life is more exciting than no life!

MIRANDA

Though Miranda is the smallest of Uranus's five major moons, it's one of the most interesting. It's made

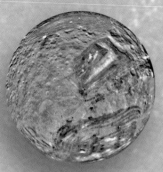

Miranda

up of a big jumble of different kinds of surfaces. There are ridges, grooves, and giant canyons. Some parts of Miranda's surface seem to have formed recently, while others are very old. Some scientists think this moon may have broken apart and re-formed as many as five times!

TITAN

Scientists think this moon has seas—but not the kind you'd want to swim in! They're probably filled with liquid ethane or methane, which are poisonous to humans. Titan is the second-largest moon in the solar system and circles around Saturn.

BLORP'S Fun Facts

If you wanted a moon of your very own, where would you look? You have lots of options! Some planets got their moons by pulling big rocks into their orbits with their gravity. Since Mars is near the asteroid belt, its two moons probably came from there. Some of Jupiter's moons may have broken into smaller pieces and formed into even more moons. Jupiter's four biggest moons formed out of leftover material when the planet itself was forming.

DACTYL

This tiny moon is only about a mile (1.5 km) across. You could walk from one side to the other in just 20 minutes. Because Dactyl has very little gravity, you could launch yourself into space using only your legs! But Dactyl doesn't orbit a planet. Instead, it orbits an **asteroid** (a giant rock that orbits the Sun in the same path as a bunch of other asteroids).

Dactyl

Titan

SHOOT FOR THE MOON

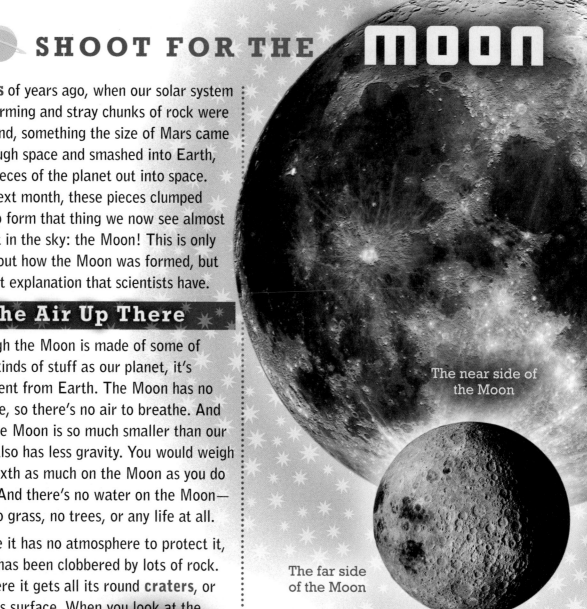

The near side of the Moon

The far side of the Moon

BILLIONS of years ago, when our solar system was still forming and stray chunks of rock were flying around, something the size of Mars came flying through space and smashed into Earth, spraying pieces of the planet out into space. Over the next month, these pieces clumped together to form that thing we now see almost every night in the sky: the Moon! This is only an idea about how the Moon was formed, but it's the best explanation that scientists have.

The Air Up There

Even though the Moon is made of some of the same kinds of stuff as our planet, it's very different from Earth. The Moon has no atmosphere, so there's no air to breathe. And because the Moon is so much smaller than our planet, it also has less gravity. You would weigh only one-sixth as much on the Moon as you do on Earth. And there's no water on the Moon—and also no grass, no trees, or any life at all.

Because it has no atmosphere to protect it, the Moon has been clobbered by lots of rock. That's where it gets all its round **craters**, or dents, in its surface. When you look at the Moon from Earth, you can also see that it has dark patches. Some people think these areas look like a face, which they call "the man in the moon." Astronomers

call these areas "seas," because they thought they looked like oceans. They formed when hot liquid rock created pools on the Moon's surface and hardened into these deep patches.

The Far Side

Sometimes you see the full, round Moon, and sometimes you can only see a tiny sliver of it. But either way, you are always seeing the same side of the Moon. As the Moon travels around Earth, it always points the same side toward our planet. Nobody knew what the far side of the Moon looked like until the spacecraft *Luna 3* took photos on its trip around the Moon in 1959. It turns out that the far side of the Moon looks a lot different from the side we see! It has a lot more craters and hardly any dark seas.

Loony Lunar Ideas

In the past, people have had all sorts of ideas about how the Moon affects us here on Earth. Some people used to think that the full Moon could make a person act crazy. The word *lunatic* comes from the Latin word for Moon, *luna*. Lunatics were people who were crazy only during a full Moon!

Nowadays, we know that the Moon can't affect the way people feel. But it does have a big effect on planet Earth. Even though the Moon's gravity is smaller compared to our planet's, it does tug on planet Earth. As the Moon travels around our planet, its gravity tugs on Earth. Because it can move easily, the water in the oceans rises up to be near the Moon. When Earth spins us into this bulge of water, we see **high tide** on Earth.

The Moon's planet-to-moon size is larger than any other planet. Because the Moon's so big, Earth and the Moon can almost be considered a double planet!

When Earth spins us out of the bulge, we see **low tide**.

As water climbs up the beach at high tide and then sinks down the beach at low tide, it leaves behind pools of water called tide pools. Scientists think life on Earth first formed in these tide pools. So we might not exist at all if it weren't for the Moon!

SPACE hall of fame

In the 1600s, Galileo used his simple telescope to discover all sorts of things that nobody knew at the time:

- The Moon is covered with craters.
- There are dark spots on the Sun, which we call **sunspots**. (Never look at the sun directly!)
- There are moons orbiting Jupiter.
- The Moon isn't a perfect sphere. It has mountains, just like Earth.

SCOTTY'S SPACE TRAVEL TIPS

The Moon would be a great place to skateboard. The gravity is only one-sixth as strong as it is on Earth. That means you and your skateboard could go six times higher than you could on Earth, so you'd have plenty of time to try all sorts of tricks in midair!

COSMIC comets

Halley's Comet

IMAGINE throwing a huge, dirty snowball really, really hard—so hard that it went into orbit around the Sun. You would have just created a **comet**! Real comets are the size of cities on Earth, and they're made of ice and dust that clumped together when the solar system was forming. Comets travel in giant orbits around the Sun. There could be as many as 100 million comets in our solar system, and each one travels on its own special path.

A Trail Through the Sky

As a comet gets close to the Sun, the ice starts to melt, and the gas and dust trail off in giant tails that can be up to 90 million miles (150 million km) long. In fact, the word *comet* comes from the Greek word *cometa*, which means "long-haired." Each time the comet passes by the Sun, parts of it trail off and the comet gets smaller and smaller. Over a long time, it will melt away completely.

When a comet passes by Earth, it can be seen in the night sky. In fact, humans have

SPACE hall of fame

The oldest record of a comet sighting is from 1059 B.C., by a Chinese astrologer.

probably been seeing comets for as long as we've walked the Earth. But even though comets seem to be glowing or even on fire, they don't actually create their own light. We can see comets because they reflect the light of the Sun (just like the Moon does), and because gas particles in the comet release energy absorbed from the Sun.

All Hail Halley!

One of the most famous comets is known as Halley's Comet. It passes by the Earth every 76 years, and it's easy to see without a telescope. Because it comes so often, some people even get to see it twice in their lifetime.

Halley's Comet

But 76 years is still a long time. If you saw a comet tomorrow and saw another comet when you were 85 years old, would you know it was the same one? It's not easy to tell comets apart. That's why even though Halley's Comet has been streaking through the night sky for centuries, it wasn't until the 1600s that Sir Edmund Halley realized it was the same comet that kept coming back! He predicted that it would return in 1758. When he was right, the comet was named after him.

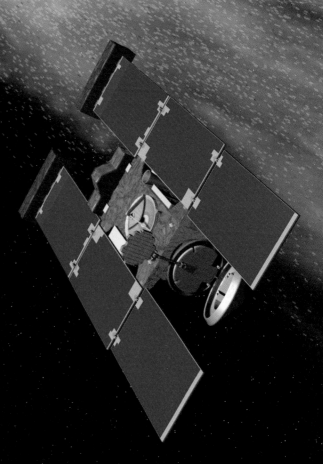

The Power Behind the Shower

When some comets pass near Earth, bits of dust from the comets' tails fall toward Earth. As this dust passes through our atmosphere, it burns up. We can see this burning dust as streaks of light in the night sky. The lights sometimes look like falling stars, but they're really called **meteors**. Some meteor showers happen at the same time every year, like the Perseid meteor shower, which happens every August when Earth passes through the trail left behind by the comet Swift-Tuttle.

Light of My Life

A capsule of comet dust landed on Earth in 2006, thanks to the work of NASA's space probe *Stardust*. This spacecraft, which was launched in 1999, visited a comet called Wild 2 (pronounced *Vilt*). There, *Stardust* captured dust particles from the comet and returned them to Earth. By studying the comet dust, scientists found that it's made of materials that are necessary for life. Life might have gotten started on Earth because the right materials were brought here by a comet, long ago!

An artist's rendering of *Stardust* encountering Wild 2

MEET THE Stars!

ALL OVER the universe, huge balls of gas are giving off tons of heat and light. From down on Earth, we can see around 1,000 of these balls every night. They're so far away that they look like teeny, tiny pinpricks of light. But each one is a star that's so big it could fit an average of *one million* Earths inside it!

The star you know best is the Sun. Even though it seems very different from the tiny dots of light you see in the night sky, those dots are just like the Sun. They're just much, much farther away. When stars form out of giant clouds of gas and dust, planets sometimes form along with them. That's how planet Earth ended up circling around the Sun. Lots of other stars have planets around them, too.

Our Sun is an average-size star. Some stars out there are much larger than the Sun. If our Sun were a kind of star called a red giant, it would spread all the way out past Earth! Fortunately for us, the Sun is just big enough and bright enough to give us daylight and warm summers.

Baby stars forming

BLORP'S Fun Facts

Have you ever held hands with a friend and spun around in a circle? Most stars in the universe do the same thing! They spin around in tight orbits with another star. These two paired-up stars are called **binary stars**. In fact, your Sun is an unusual star because it's alone.

✶ Great Balls of Fire! ✶

Some people draw stars with five points. That's because the stars in the sky can *look* like spiky, twinkling dots. But really, all stars, including the Sun, are big round balls. They only look like they have spikes because Earth's atmosphere changes the way the light looks when it reaches your eyes.

Like marbles, stars come in lots of different sizes and colors. Small, young stars are very hot and bright blue. Big, older stars are cooler and look red. When you look at the night sky, it might seem like all the stars are white, but as you let your eyes adjust to the darkness, you might be able to make out the different colors. Stars can look red, orange, yellow, white, and blue.

Holy-Moly!

When really, really big stars (made up of ten or 15 times more gas than our Sun) get old, they explode in giant bursts called **supernovas.**

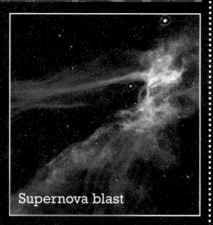
Supernova blast

The outer layer of the star is thrown outward in the explosion. The core of the star falls in on itself into a teeny-tiny point containing tons and tons of material. This point has gravity that's so strong that even light can't escape it! It's almost like a hole in the universe, which is why scientists call these dead stars **black holes.**

POP CULTURE

In the 2005 movie *Zathura*, the space-themed board game that Walter and Danny are playing suddenly becomes real, sending them out into space. The game ends only when they are sucked into a black hole. If somebody was really sucked into a black hole, it definitely wouldn't work like it did in the movie. It sent Walter and Danny back home safe and sound!

An artist's picture of a black hole tearing apart a star and consuming part of it

SUNNY DAYS

IF YOU TOOK all the planets and moons in our solar system and squeezed them together into a big ball, that ball would still be much smaller than the Sun. Even though the Sun is only a medium-size star, it's a superstar in our solar system! Without the Sun's gravity, the planets wouldn't stay in orbit. And without the Sun's heat and light, we wouldn't be able to live on Earth.

Bouncing and Banging

Inside our Sun, tiny particles called **atoms** bounce around really, really fast. Sometimes, when two atoms smash into each other, they join together. When this happens, a lot of energy gets released. Some of this energy is in the form of heat and light, and it travels out of the Sun in all directions. A tiny amount of that light hits Earth. It only takes light eight minutes to get from the Sun to us. But this light can get banged around inside the Sun for tens of millions of years before it makes it to the surface and gets free.

Hit the Spot

When you get bitten by a mosquito, you get an itchy red bump on your skin that usually lasts for a week or two and then goes away. You have something in common with the Sun! **Sunspots** are dark spots on the Sun that usually last a couple of weeks, although sometimes they can last for months (like a mosquito bite you keep scratching). A sunspot is kind of like a storm on the surface of the sun. Sunspots look dark because they're cooler than the rest of the Sun's surface. They're small compared to the rest of the Sun, but they can be several times bigger than planet Earth!

Fantastic Flare

Sometimes big explosions happen on the Sun near sunspots. These are called **solar flares**, and they're the biggest explosions in the solar system. Solar flares can build up for hours or

BLORP'S Fun Facts

The line that separates our solar system from the rest of space is called the **heliopause**. That's the place where particles from the Sun meet particles from the rest of the universe. Nobody's sure how far away the heliopause is, but it's probably more than 100 times farther from the Sun than planet Earth.

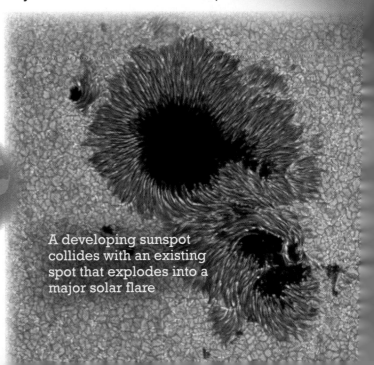

A developing sunspot collides with an existing spot that explodes into a major solar flare

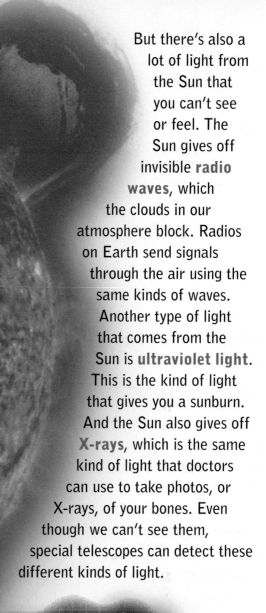

But there's also a lot of light from the Sun that you can't see or feel. The Sun gives off invisible **radio waves**, which the clouds in our atmosphere block. Radios on Earth send signals through the air using the same kinds of waves. Another type of light that comes from the Sun is **ultraviolet light**. This is the kind of light that gives you a sunburn. And the Sun also gives off **X-rays**, which is the same kind of light that doctors can use to take photos, or X-rays, of your bones. Even though we can't see them, special telescopes can detect these different kinds of light.

MEASURING UP

If the Sun were shrunk down to the size of your head, Earth would be only about as big as one of your pupils!

even days, but the explosions happen in just a few minutes. The energy that comes from them can affect satellites and radio signals on our planet.

✳ Looking at Light ✳

The Sun gives off energy in the form of light. You can see a lot of the light, and you can feel some of the light. (Here's a hint: It feels hot!)

CLOUDS

WITH RAINBOW LININGS

NGC 1999

YOU MAY HAVE HEARD that "every cloud has a silver lining." But the huge clouds of gas and dust out in space actually have linings that are blue, red, pink, and purple. These clouds are called **nebulae** (NEB-you-lay), and they can take all different shapes, just like the clouds in our sky.

Over time, the glowing gas and dust in a nebula can get pulled together by gravity and start to spin. As it squeezes together, the atoms in the center start hitting one another so hard that they stick together, start releasing energy, and then a star is formed.

A Key to the Sky

The nebula above, known as NGC 1999, appears to have a keyhole in the middle of it. But that dark area is really a cloud of gas and dust in front of the bright nebula, blocking all of its light. NGC 1999 is a **reflection nebula**. It glows because it reflects light from nearby stars, just like fog around a streetlamp on a misty night.

Thor's Helmet Nebula

Butterfly Nebula

✶ Wings and Things ✶

◅ Some people call this nebula Thor's Helmet. Other people called it the Duck Nebula. Which does it look like to you? Either way, this nebula appears to have wings because particles streaming out from a massive star nearby are pushing its gas and dust away.

SPACE hall of fame

Charles Messier, an astronomer in the 1700s, devoted his life to the search for comets. He kept finding bright, fuzzy objects that looked like comets but didn't move across the sky. He made a catalog of about 100 of these mystery objects.

It turns out that a lot of them were nebulae! Astronomers still use many of the numbers Messier gave them. The Crab Nebula is also named "M1," or "Messier 1."

◅ This nebula is nicknamed the Butterfly Nebula, because the clouds on either side look like butterfly wings. These clouds of gas and dust are red because particles inside them give off red light. Nebulae that create and give off their own light are called **emission nebulae**.

SWIRLS & WHIRLS OF stars

WHAT DO YOU GET when you add together 100 million stars, throw in a whole bunch of nebulae, sprinkle around more gas and dust, add a huge black hole (or two), and mix it all together? You get a **galaxy**! Galaxies are enormous clumps of stars, gas, and dust, all held together by gravity.

✷ All Shapes and Sizes ✷

Like everything else out in space, galaxies come in all different shapes and sizes. Some look like spirals, and others look like round or squashed balls. You already learned about the galaxy you live in, the Milky Way. We think it's just one of many **spiral galaxies** out there. Spiral galaxies are shaped like discs and look like pinwheels, with arms that wind outward as the galaxy rotates. Spiral galaxies usually contain middle-aged stars and lots of gas and dust. ∨

Elliptical galaxy

Galaxies that are shaped like squashed balls are called **elliptical galaxies**. These round galaxies usually have older stars and only a little gas and dust. Because they don't have a clear shape and don't have much gas and dust, these galaxies don't look as interesting from our perspective down here on Earth.

But what do you call a galaxy that's lumpy, or bumpy, or long and skinny? Some galaxies don't seem to have a clear shape. These are called **irregular galaxies**. ∨

Spiral galaxy

Irregular galaxy

SCOTTY'S SPACE TRAVEL TIPS

We think that we live in a spiral galaxy, but we can't be sure, because we've never been outside our galaxy to look back at it! If you make it that far away, you should check for us!

Coma Cluster

✴ A Crash Course

You learned that even when you're sitting still, the planet you live on is traveling around the solar system. But planets and moons aren't the only things in the universe that are traveling. Entire galaxies move around in space, pulled by the gravitational force of other stuff out there.

Sometimes, two galaxies are pulled toward each other. Very, very slowly, over hundreds of millions of years, the galaxies crash into each other. The shape of each galaxy will be torn apart, as the stars, gas, and dust inside get pulled in new directions. It might sound scary, but in fact, when galaxies collide, usually the stars inside the galaxies don't run into each other. That's because there's so much empty space between every single star.

It's different for the clouds of gas and dust that make up each galaxy. This stuff takes up a lot of space in each galaxy, so it runs into other clouds of gas and dust when galaxies collide. When this happens, clouds of gas can get pushed together with so much force that new stars are born!

Great Gobs of Galaxies

Most spiral galaxies are out in space on their own or with small groups of other galaxies. But elliptical galaxies usually clump together in great gobs of galaxies called **clusters**.

One of the most crowded clusters we know of is called the Coma Cluster. Thousands of galaxies are packed into this cluster—and every single one of them contains billions of stars. The closest major galaxy cluster to us is called the Virgo Cluster. It's so huge that it pulls other galaxies and groups of galaxies toward it—including our Milky Way Galaxy! Eventually, the galaxies that Virgo pulls toward it will become part of its cluster. Red rover, red rover, send the Milky Way right over!

BLORP'S Fun Facts

Blorp! Galaxies are surrounded by invisible stuff called **dark matter**. We only know it's there because we can see it tug on the rest of the galaxy with its gravity. There's probably much more invisible dark matter in the universe than stuff we can see!

THE galaxy GALLERY

WE CAN'T send a telescope outside of the Milky Way Galaxy to see what it looks like from the outside, so astronomers can only guess what our galaxy is shaped like. Studying other galaxies far beyond our own helps them understand what it might look like. Check out some examples!

Raising the Bar

The galaxy known as NGC 7479 is called a "barred" spiral galaxy. That's because it has a bar across its center. The arms of the galaxy spiral out from the bar. ⋎

Barred spiral galaxy

Spinning the Pinwheel

The Pinwheel Galaxy is a beautiful spiral. It's so large that its gravity pulls on galaxies nearby. ⋎

Pinwheel Galaxy

Try This Hat on for Size!

Like a coin, spiral galaxies look round when seen from their flat sides, but they're very thin when seen from the edge. The Sombrero Galaxy is a spiral galaxy whose edge faces us. If we could see it from another angle, it might look similar to the Pinwheel Galaxy. But from our view here on Earth, it looks like a wide-brimmed hat called a *sombrero*. ➤

Antennae Galaxies

The Tadpole Galaxy is *almost* a normal spiral galaxy, but something happened to it to drag a bunch of its stars out into a long tail. Some astronomers think a smaller galaxy nearby was swung around the Tadpole Galaxy by the Tadpole's huge force of gravity, and the smaller galaxy pulled the Tadpole's tail away. Just as tadpoles on Earth lose their tails when they grow up, this Tadpole will probably lose its tail eventually, too. The stars in its tail will break off and form their own clusters.

Putting Out Feelers

Is that an insect with antennae out there in the sky? Some astronomers called these two crashing galaxies the Antennae Galaxies, because together they look like a bug with two antennae out in front of it. The antennae were formed when the gravity of the two galaxies pushed and pulled at the stuff inside the galaxies, sending it flying.

Tadpole Galaxy

Sombrero Galaxy

SPACE hall of fame

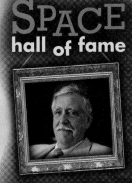

Some galaxies just don't fit in. That's what astronomer Dr. Halton C. Arp discovered. In 1966, he made a list of all the weird galaxies he saw in the *Atlas of Peculiar Galaxies*. The Pinwheel Galaxy and the Tadpole Galaxy were both on his list. Later, astronomers found that a lot of the galaxies he included are weird because they're being tugged on by other galaxies. Hey, imagine what you'd look like if you had a galaxy tugging at your sleeve!

mission ACCOMPLISHED!

YOU'VE TRAVELED all over the universe, from the closest planet to the most far-out cloud of gas and dust. Which parts do you want to go back and visit? With the books in the **Ultimate Space Club**, you'll get a closer look at all of it. You'll also learn more about what it's like to travel and even live in space. And you'll find out whether there could be anything else alive traveling or living somewhere in the universe!

With each new Ultimate Space Club book, you'll also get a cool new Space Kit. So keep one eye on the stars and your other eye on your mailbox!

And stay tuned for the next episode in our *Ultimate Space Race* adventure!